STONE
SETTING

STONE SETTING

Scott McIntyre

 THE CROWOOD PRESS

First published in 2020 by
The Crowood Press Ltd
Ramsbury, Marlborough
Wiltshire SN8 2HR

enquiries@crowood.com
www.crowood.com

This impression 2024

British Library Cataloguing-in-Publication Data
A catalogue record for this book is available from the British Library.

ISBN 978 1 78500 691 3

Cover image
Diamond Stacking Rings by Scott McIntyre, photo by Vanilla Ink.

Frontispiece
Vanilla Ink 'Parabola' ring. The angled, carved arcs of this ring are the perfect setting for the deep greens of the pear shape. The flourish of 9ct rose gold blends everything together to create a stunning bezel set piece. (Stacey Bentley)

Line illustrations by Jennifer Colquhoun.

Typeset by Jean Cussons Typesetting, Diss, Norfolk

Printed and bound in India by Thomson Press India ltd

CONTENTS

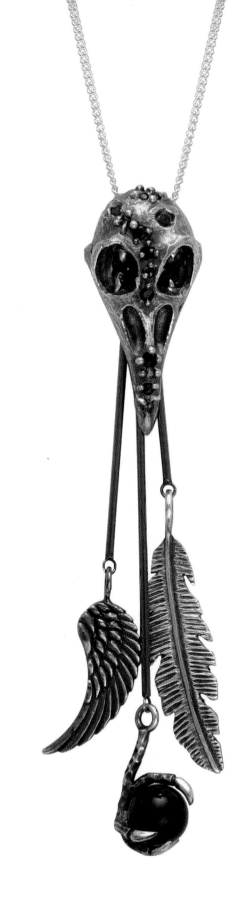

PREFACE

The inside pages of this book are like a glimpse into a hidden world in the inside of my head. No, don't let this put you off, we're only looking at the professional contents, not anything weird or scary. I've been a goldsmith for some thirty years now. Along my jewellery journey, I have listened, watched, made mistakes, finely tuned, invented and executed a wide range of techniques and methods relating to stone setting.

At times, it may have felt like I was going nowhere, stuck in a rut, frustrated and confused about new techniques and the intense pressure that was forced upon me. However, I persisted, persevered and pushed on through like a true force of nature. I am, and always have been quite tenacious, something which has helped me to become the craftsman that I am today. Add to that an abundance of natural skill and a whack of autism, and you've pretty much got the perfect jeweller!

It's high time that the wealth of knowledge I have gathered was put down into print and made good use of. It took me a little while into my career before I realized that I had been blessed with an incredibly high level of training.

My apprenticeship was tough, often being thrown in at the deep end and being asked to perform unfamiliar tasks both quickly and efficiently. Little by little, I learned and improved.

LEFT: **Vanilla Ink – 'The Guardian Raven'. Vanilla Ink's first foray into casting with stones in place was an epic success. Created in collaboration with Circinn Studios, the sterling silver and blue sapphire pendant is a visually striking piece of jewellery that reveals further detail the closer you look at it. (Stacey Bentley)**

I always believed that every jeweller learned this way and received similar content with their training. How far from the truth I was. My jewellery education was, and still is, bordering on unique. There are not a lot of goldsmiths out there who received that amount of training and with such intensity. I am forever grateful for my opportunity when I was just a young thing. I never appreciated it then, but I sure do now.

It took a long time for me to realize just how blessed I was. It was only when I started to believe in my own abilities (despite some harsh tactics by some employers – negative and highly critical training never works, something I strongly believe in) that it became clear I had some talents. It would have been easy to acquiesce into the world I was in, but I felt there was more I could offer.

With my moment of epiphany came the desire to teach and pass on my skills. I don't believe in hoarding all these tips and tricks for myself, I would much rather someone else benefitted from my knowledge, and in turn, passed it on to someone else. I know of some places that treat their techniques as some form of classified top secret, never revealing them and sticking with the myth that their way is the best way. Some might say that these workshops are successful and that their methods are justified, but it just doesn't sit right with me. We're a niche profession, and highly skilled goldsmiths and setters are few and far between. It feels right that we should nurture the community and do our best to ensure that the future of jewellery is bright. It took me a while, but now that's what I do in my day-to-day life. It's good to be free!

In 2017, I took a leap of faith and founded Vanilla Ink Jewellery School. This felt like the final piece of the puzzle was in place, and now a bright light shone straight up in the sky! Between the force of nature that is our team, we can devote our careers to both professional and skills development, while focusing on giving as many jewellers and silversmiths as possible a place to be educated, inspired, and empowered. Every day I am grateful for that opportunity, and I'm not sure any of us realized just what a force we could be. We have a masterplan to do our best within the industry, and we aim to see it through.

Who is this book for?

Believe it or not, this book is for you! I'm assuming you're a jeweller or silversmith, and now you want to stone set? Welcome to the club! We don't get jackets, sadly (but we *can* sell you an apron). The jewellery world is a funny one. It

is a rare thing indeed to come across a jeweller who is a jack of all trades. There are too many sub-categories to allow complete mastery of them all.

There are designers, mounters, setters and polishers. Throw in wax carving, casting, plating, enamelling, electroforming, engraving, the list goes on. I myself have been lucky to master a fair few of these techniques, one in particular being stone setting.

This manual is a visual representation of my career. It is not your average stone setting guide. It is not dull, mundane or thin on content. It is written with the intention to connect with you, to make you feel comfortable, to feel like I'm almost there with you, guiding through your journey. It is a stone setting manual that stands out from the rest, simply because it intends to integrate with you, your skill level and your attitude. Books like these are great for

Vanilla Ink – Various commissions. A few examples of the variety of jewellery designed, created and manufactured by Vanilla Ink. Each piece is made in close collaboration with the client to ensure they not only receive exactly what they want but feel immersed within the process. (Vanilla Ink)

Vanilla Ink – Solitaire Ring. Vanilla Ink can create designs ranging from epic to classic, the sublime to the ridiculous! This particular ring was made in platinum and claw set with a 0.4ct sparkling brown diamond. Simple, yet effective, and most definitely with added signature work. (Vanilla Ink)

students, they are painfully constructed to help you along your way and hopefully become a better goldsmith. But this one wants to talk to you. A student simply cannot learn if they are not engaged with their tutor. In this case, I am your tutor. I want you to feel relaxed, comfortable and ready to learn. We'll do it our way, stand out from the crowd, and make you into a demon at your craft in no time.

And so you join me on the journey to become a setter. What do you need? Good hand skills? Coordination? Patience? Well, yes, these are all handy. Try having a level head, a desire to learn, and a great deal of patience and persistence. These are all good qualities. But most importantly, an understanding that to learn and move forward, you will fail, over and over again, until you get it right. You will not become a setter overnight, and nor will

you become one with a flippant attitude. You must be prepared for the frustration, the pain, the sore hands and shoulders. Sometimes you want to yell into the void and wonder where did it all go wrong? But the reward? It's incredible! The sense of achievement felt, the thrill of seeing the complex tasks you've just nailed, the joy, contentment and gratitude of the client when they receive their job. That's what it's all about!

We mounters and setters are the engine room of the jewellery industry. We exist in the grimy, dusty, messy and sometimes painful backrooms of glamorous jewellery shops. We do our job for personal satisfaction, knowing we've made someone incredibly happy yet again. It's not the accolades and awards or the glory, it's because we're good at it and because we can.

Want to be part of that? Let's go learning.

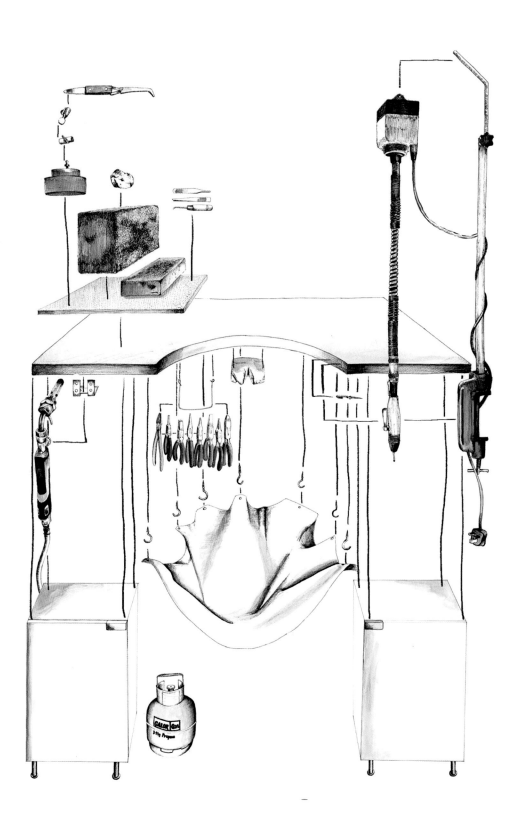

PREPARATION IS KEY

As with all craft, you can't just rock up to the jeweller's bench, sit down and begin to stone set. Thought, planning and a great deal of respect for the art must be considered before you commence your journey. If you take all this on board before everything else, then you'll have a good basis to begin learning. You can't skip stages or you'll miss vital techniques. This has to be applied when it comes to preparation, too. It's not a good start to be cocky and leap straight into stone setting without prior thought, as it could lead to injury or premature wear and tear on your precious body. All around the world, there are jewellers at the beginning of an amazing journey. But we only have one body, and it's incredibly important to take care of it.

The Bench

Jeweller's benches come in all shapes and sizes. From the handmade to the ones bought from jewellery suppliers, it's a sure-fire bet that no two will look or feel the same. A bench must be tailored to fit your needs, with height, width and storage all becoming a factor.

A hobbyist or beginner jeweller may start their journey at a kitchen table or office desk, but as they become more serious about their craft, a jeweller must consider investing in a proper, solid, more professional-feeling bench.

As a stone setter, tools must be within easy reach. There is no point in having to get up to walk to the other side of the workshop for a tool when you are knee-deep in intricate work. It breaks your momentum, concentration and rhythm. Whichever tool you use to clamp or hold your setting job in, it's incredibly important that your other hand be free to reach around your bench and find that vital tool you need at the trickiest of moments.

Think about this when you are seated at your bench. Where are your push tools, your burnishers, your loupe? Can you reach them while seated? Are all of your burrs located close by? Do your scorpers live in a drawer right beside you? Is your sharpening stone handy? Start off by indulging in some Feng Shui! Find the balance and work out a layout that is best for you.

I have two cupboards either side of me, with each having a selection of drawers and boxes. Both are clearly labelled so that I'm not spending ages figuring out what is where. On my bench surface, more vital tools are within easy reach. Burrs are kept in a handy pot, as are flush setting tools and grain tools. Saw blades are easily identifiable by size and again, within my range. If you get into this habit of keeping things at close quarters, you'll become a slicker, faster stone setter in no time!

LEFT: **The jeweller's bench. Benches can vary in looks and sizes, but there are some constants that will cross over to all stone setters. Here we see Scott's bench in 'exploded' form, showing how all major parts fit together. (Jenni Colquhoun)**

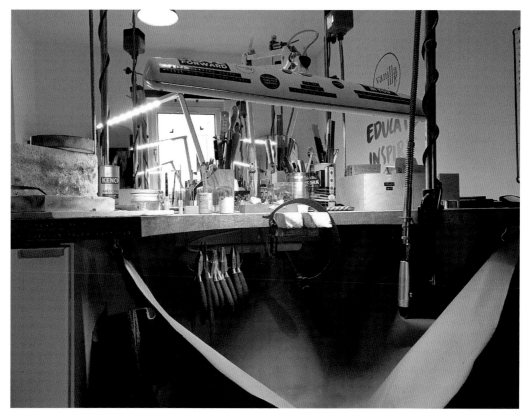

Scott's bench. The sight Scott sees almost every day. Although there will be slight discrepancies between all jeweller's benches, some things remain the same – a bench peg, a skin to catch scrap and an abundance of tools make this a familiar view for lots of jewellers. (Vanilla Ink)

The Tools Required

You will find a more comprehensive Glossary of Terms towards the back of this book, but I wanted to quickly run through the most vital of tools you will need for stone setting. Not only do you need a strong, sturdy bench, but a decent bench peg is also key. These come in various shapes and sizes, with each one being tailored to each jeweller's individual needs. Modern technology allows us to use fancy bench pegs and clamps, alongside all-singing, all-dancing microscopes and lenses. This manual, however, is aimed at those of you beginning your stone setting journey. Modern-day setting tools are incredible and can really enhance a stone setter's abilities but at a price. Literally.

Tools like these are expensive and for most beginners, unobtainable. This is why I like to teach the good old-fashioned way so that it's a level playing field for everyone. After all, if you learn on the acoustic guitar, then the electric guitar will be a doddle! At Vanilla Ink, we teach traditional methods using rudimentary tools. This way, the student can leave the workshop and begin to stone set with a basic budget. There is no point in jewellers coming to class, only for their dreams of becoming a stone setter to be crushed when they realize the kit required is beyond them.

I myself do not use any of the modern equipment. I think it is important to show students that high-level, top-class results are achievable with the simplest of equipment. This

Up close and personal with Scott's bench peg. Not quite a traditional bench peg, the 45-degree sloping face allows for jobs to be held up against it, making it easier and quicker to get the job done. Note the natural grooves and shapes created by the jeweller. Each person will eventually style a bench peg in their own, unique way. It's almost like art in itself! (Vanilla Ink)

helps them to understand that the only thing between them and being a high-end setter is time and practice. A lot of practice!

Preparation and Maintenance

Now that you've gathered an arsenal of stone setting tools and equipment, you need to look after them. While this is the rule for all of your tools, it is especially important to correctly set up and maintain stone setting tools. There are a number of reasons for this.

Tools can be expensive. In that respect, we need to protect, nurture and prevent any damage. Think of them as your children! These tools will become part of you, what you do and the pieces you create. They become precious to you and they will be missed when they're gone. I still have my first worn bench peg in a drawer at home somewhere alongside some of my favourite tools that are now past their sell-by date! They created some of my favourite pieces and it's hard to let them go!

A poorly looked-after tool becomes economical folly. If you mistreat or break it due to lack of care, then you pay out some more of your hard-earned cash sooner than you planned. Sharpen gravers properly, lubricate burrs and drills, clean perishable materials with the appropriate solutions. The more life you can squeeze out of your tools, the more economical you can be.

Don't allow them to fade away without getting proper use from them.

More important, however, is the prevention of injury. A stone setter's fingers, hands and arms will be battle-scarred by injuries from the past, from the serious gouge to a scratch. As we say here at Vanilla Ink, 'There will be blood each week,' which is true for most setters. Carelessness can be a factor, as is simple bad luck, but the most common is using poorly prepared tools.

THE TOOLS REQUIRED FOR STONE SETTING

If you don't have all of these, you may not manage to carry out all forms of stone setting. But not to worry, you'll add to your collection as you go along. And let's not run before we can walk! Start off with the most basic forms of setting, which require the least amount of tools. Techniques are transferable between basic and more advanced styles anyway, so you can accumulate as you progress.

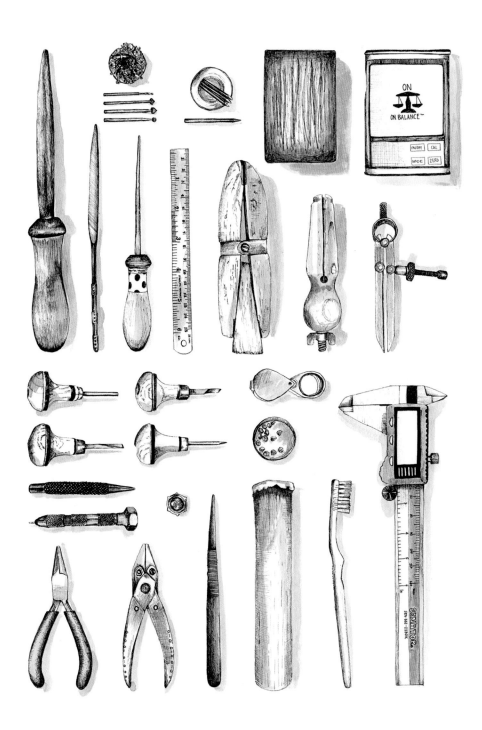

The tools required. A pretty comprehensive illustration, which catalogues every tool you will need to become a stone setter and work your way through this manual. When it's laid out like this, you see exactly what's required and how achievable it could actually be for you. (Jennifer Colquhoun)

Various scorpers with sharpening stones. Some scorpers and gravers are colour coded at Vanilla Ink so the students can identify them easily. At the beginning of their journey, it's often simpler to identify them as blue or red until the student recognizes them by name alone. (Vanilla Ink)

Contrary to popular belief, a blunt tool will cause far more damage than a beautifully sharp one (you can ask kitchen chefs for verification here). Blunt tools can slip, slide and tear into all sorts of places. But just because they aren't sharp enough for cutting metal, they can still pierce your soft skin with great ease.

When I teach, I say that most, if not all, of my worst injuries have come from stupidity. Being careless, cocky or hasty will not work out well for you. 'Don't be an idiot like me,' I tell my students, pointing out my scars. 'Think about what you are doing,' I always finish with. I have been very fortunate with injuries, with a few stitches here and there, but I've known jewellers who have really hurt themselves. And every time, they have lamented their lack of thought, preparation, and cursed their haste. Think about it and you'll be fine.

Sharpening scorpers

To be a stone setter, you need to be able to prepare and maintain your scorpers and gravers. It's important to learn this fast, as scorpers blunt often and quickly. Another thing to take on board is that whatever finish you apply to the scorper's cutting surface, the very same finish will be applied to the metal. It takes a little bit of skill to know how to use various sharpening stones and silicones to achieve an ultra-high polish which cuts beautifully through metal.

How to do it
When you first receive a new scorper, it's far too long. The first thing you'll need to do is grind it to the length you need. Everyone's hand is different; you'll eventually know the ideal size

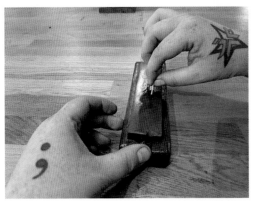

Sharpening a scorper. The preparation and maintenance of scorpers can seem fearsome due to the fast whirring of the grinder coupled with the deluge of sparks created. Once you get used it, it's a relatively simple process. Note the shallow angle on the scorper face, as well as the correct hand position to grind a sharp edge. (Vanilla Ink)

(obviously bear in mind that each time you sharpen, the shorter it becomes). Taper the end so that you can hammer it into your favourite shape of handle. (I prefer the mushroom shape, it has a flat on it which prevents it from rolling off your bench.) Then you can begin to shape the end.

It has to taper gently down so that the cutting face is small. The more surface you have to constantly sharpen, the more difficult it will be to maintain. From the side, it should look like a very shallow ski slope, gently sweeping down to almost a point. Use your grinding wheel with care and skill. Sparks will literally fly, making it look quite spectacular! The one thing to remember is to constantly dip the end you are sharpening in water to cool it down. It is very easy to overheat the tip of a scorper, as once it goes blue, it's gone. It is brittle and useless and has to be ground away.

Once you've used the grinder to achieve the correct shape, it's now onto using various sharpening stones to get the correct finish on it. I use a pre-oiled India stone to do the heavy lifting, then move onto an Arkansas stone to get a nice, bright finish. To get an ultra-bright finish, use a firm silicone wheel in your pendant drill. This may take a little getting used to but is really worth it.

How to sit

To me, this is vital for not only stone setters but all jewellers. Time and time again, I have seen pictures of jewellers at the bench or visited workshops where the layout has made me shudder. Benches are often too low, meaning the jeweller is stooped over their work. I cringe at the prospect of their future back pain, meaning their career could be cut short or their posture damaged forever. How to sit is often overlooked, casually tossed to the side as unimportant, but it is the most important thing you'll do at the bench. Get it right at the start, and it will become second nature within no time.

When I first walked into a jeweller's workshop for my job interview, I was thrown in at the deep end – I was to sit a bench test before any questions being answered! The first thing I noticed, and I can still see this in my mind's eye, is that the goldsmiths were sitting preposterously low. It looked odd, completely unnatural and almost

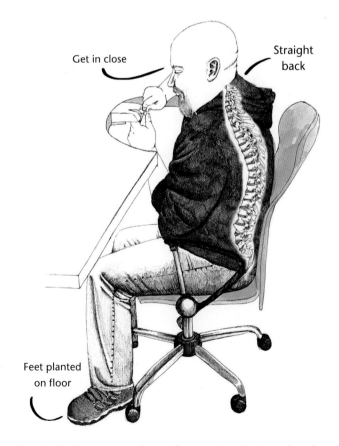

Get in close

Straight back

Feet planted on floor

How to sit. Here we see the perfect way to sit at your bench. Straight back, no hunching, feet on the floor, eyes close to the job. Note the height of the bench in relation to the shoulders. (Jennifer Colquhoun)

comedic. However, it was swiftly pointed out that a jeweller must not hunch over towards their bench peg, the job must almost be at their nose, with feet firmly planted on the floor.

A good rule to live by is to sit in your chair (comfortable, adjustable with a good back to it) and look at where your shoulder is in relation to the top of the bench. The ideal position is to have the top of the shoulder poking up an inch or two above the bench surface. I will guarantee that this may be news to most of you but believe me when I say it will prevent a lot of back problems in the future. Us setters take a great deal of punishment across the top of the shoulders and down the back; we must include self-care within our daily schedule.

Where is your bench peg in relation to your face? Lean in slightly; if you have to look too far down or you are looming over it, you are too high. Remember, you are not sitting down for

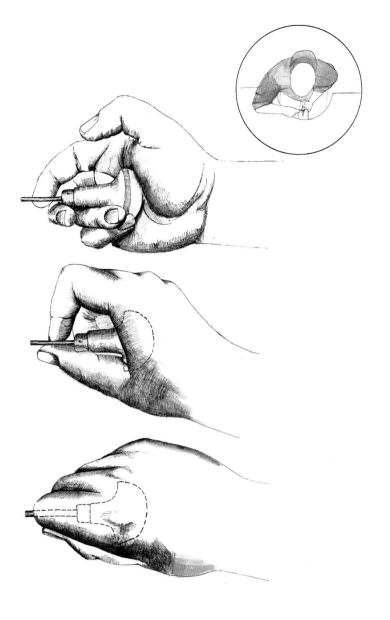

**Basic technique.
(Jennifer
Colquhoun)**

a lovely meal. The benchtop is not to be just above your lap so you can tuck into something tasty, it's raised higher to reduce fatigue and increase ease of access.

Feet *must* be planted on the floor. If I see anyone sitting with crossed legs in my workshop, it is pointed out and adjusted swiftly! Continuation to do so will result in public humiliation! You are not sitting watching television at home – you are a professional performing a skilled and intense job. We must take it seriously. It is vital that we listen up to those who have had long and successful careers. They know how to treat their bodies and will pass on the care required.

Live by these rules and you have a good basis to start becoming a jeweller and stone setter. It may seem overly pedantic, but you'll thank me for it decades down the line.

Basic Technique

We continue with some more vital instructions and important rules. The basic technique crosses over all forms of setting, from claw to pavé, bezel to channel. Once explained, it makes a great deal of sense. When I teach this part in class, I make sure that each student knows the importance of it. I go into great detail and use analogies and physical examples. I feel that this part is chronically under-taught, which leads to students becoming frustrated and possibly giving up. Setters are becoming increasingly rare animals: I'd rather we didn't become extinct due to something easily fixable.

We have already established how to sit, let's move to more intricate details. Let's start with the way we hold a push tool. Everybody's hands are a different shape; we'll acknowledge that from the start. This means that your push tools, which become an extension of you and your abilities, must be tailored to fit. This may take a while but you'll eventually settle on one or two pushers that will be your best pals for years. Find a handle shape that nestles nicely in your palm. Now close your fingers around it. The length of the actual pusher now is down to the individual. Try out a few different ones until you settle on a length you are comfortable with.

The handle in your palm must point straight up towards your elbow. This creates a sort of piston, which becomes a vital source of power for setting. The main power, however, comes from your core and your shoulder. The most important thing is that you do not try to push from the wrist. This will get you nowhere. It is the most common source of failure and one that needs to be nipped in the bud immediately.

Think of a boxer performing a right hook. The movement comes from the core, right in the centre of their chest. The shoulder moves simultaneously, rocking forward in unison, the process coming from the core with a stiff, locked shoulder. This, coupled with the 'piston' you have created down at the business end of your arm, drives everything towards the metal in a powerful, short, sharp movement. It is essential that you take the time to master this technique and use it as your default way to set. It crosses over so many styles and is used in similar ways for more advanced methods.

It may take you a while to become accustomed to this. It can also seem confusing from just words and diagrams, or even actually watching someone teach it. But with enough practice, it will eventually fall into place and all will become clear. It's like a true moment of clarity!

BEZEL AND CLAW SETTING

Bezel Setting

Bezel setting is probably the oldest and earliest known way of setting a stone into jewellery. Its theory is simple; create a wall of metal in which the stone sits, then push the wall over the stone until it is secure. The style is known by various different names, including rubover, tube and collet. However, in my opinion, each of these names means pretty much exactly the same thing.

For example, just because you used a piece of tube to set your stone in, it doesn't necessarily mean it is entirely tube setting. You still *rubbed over the bezel*, didn't you? Which is also a *collet*. Complicated, isn't it? This leads to confusion and misunderstandings amongst students or jewellers beginning their jewellery journey.

I'm sure you will find setters out there who are sticklers for the rules and would define certain things in specific ways, but sometimes simplifying things can make life a lot easier. And for the purposes of this manual, let's just refer to bezel setting as a broad definition across the board.

LEFT: **Shimell & Madden – Tanzanite and diamond pendant. This stunning yellow gold pendant shows how to mix setting styles and different stones beautifully. While the tanzanite is the star of the show, the whole look is complemented by the bezel set diamond at the bottom of the piece. (Shimell & Madden)**

Theory

As previously mentioned, bezel setting is the art of creating and pushing a wall over a stone. This can mean any stone, whether it be cabochon or faceted. A lot of students ask me to teach them how to set cabs. I tell them that once they know how to set cabs, then they know how to set faceted as well. Create a wall, create a seat, sit the stone, set the stone. This principle works for all stones. We need to stop splitting things up, creating more categories, complicating things for the beginner. There is plenty of time to refine your skills as your technique grows. For now, as this is a manual designed for learning, let's keep things simple.

Different techniques

On our full day Bezel Setting Class at Vanilla Ink, we take a look at three different ways of setting. The first (and simplest) is using pre-formed tube, taking a burr, then setting the stone. This introduces the students to the previously discussed way to sit, the correct technique for setting, and the most rudimentary way to bezel set a stone.

Next up, we create a bezel from a strip of metal, solder onto a backplate, then set as before. Finally, we use tube again, but this time, instead of burring into the walls of the tube, we create a seat for the stone ourselves and solder it in place. These are the three most common ways you will bezel set, with it being very unusual for you to do anything different.

'Granite' ring. Peter Gilroy's stunning use of texture and mixed metals are used perfectly to enhance this belter of a diamond. Each aspect complements the others fantastically. (Peter W. Gilroy)

Using tube

Your local friendly bullion supplier will provide with you all forms of tube in a wide range of dimensions, ready to be cut and used for setting. This can prove economical, both financially and time-wise, as the pre-made settings are all ready and waiting to be sliced into their appropriate size.

For the purposes of these techniques, let's assume you are making a simple pendant, which will require placing your job into a dop stick.

Creating a bezel from metal strip

Using this method, you are in control of the dimensions. Creating your own bezels is an essential skill, as ready-made tube or settings are not always available. Making round bezels is a good starting point for making shaped ones. The process is slightly trickier, but starting here will get you used to the fine margins required. If you make the bezel too big, the stone will rattle around inside and prove difficult to secure. Too small and it simply won't fit!

Creating a seat within the bezel

The third technique in our thrilling instalment is very similar to the first method, only this time instead of cutting into the wall of the setting, we create a seat for it, or bearer wire (call it whatever you want, sometimes names don't matter). This means that our outer wall doesn't have to be quite as thick as when we burr into it. Our setting depth can be reduced as the stone should slide sweetly into place, sitting on its little seat. Alternatively, you can keep a thicker wall and use it to give a bold appearance to the overall setting. This strong, wide tube setting proves popular and can be used to make a smaller stone look a little bigger.

Before you start

Although there are multiple ways to seat the stone (this is quite common for stone setting), the basic method for setting remains a constant. No matter what kind of stone we are setting,

McCaul Goldsmiths – 18ct yellow gold diamond 'Twist' ring. Bezel setting with a literal twist! McCaul's elegant yellow gold ring is an ideal home for the beautiful rose cut stone. (Keith Leighton)

whether it be cabochon or faceted, and regardless of how and where the stone sits, the ultimate aim is to push the setting wall over the stone. That's what it boils down to. The following instructions assume that you have previously manufactured the mount or setting and are all ready to go.

keep reading! Take a setting burr (5mm for a 5mm stone and so on) and gently cut a seat for each stone. Go slow. You don't want to cut down too far. Make sure you always use a lube of some sort (we just use good old 3-in-1 oil). This makes burring easier and prolongs the life of the burr.

Method

Step 1

Have your piece ready to go. This can either be in a dop stick with setter's wax or Thermo-Loc, your ring clamp or indeed whatever you use to keep items in place. Just ensure that the piece is rock solid and won't fly off when pushing. This is how we hurt ourselves and nobody wants to kick off their stone setting career with blood.

Step 2

If you have created the bezel for the stone to sit in, skip further down. If you have to cut a seat,

'Nova' ring. Clean lines and crisp execution make Shimell & Madden's Nova ring stand out from the crowd. (Shimell & Madden)

Step 3

Check every now and then to see where the stone sits. If it isn't low enough, burr some more. If it isn't going in at all, you may have to wiggle your burr a little outwards to allow the stone to slot in. Sometimes a stone can be 4.05mm, which requires a little bit of extra work with a 4mm setting burr.

Step 4

Remember, at this level of precision, as little as 0.01mm can make a difference! You want the table of the stone to sit approximately just above the surface of the metal. However, this can be a very vague rule. A larger stone (say 10mm for example) has a much larger distance between girdle and table. If we were to apply the rule, there would be far too much metal to push over. There is no golden law about how far to seat a bezel setting, it is something that simply becomes learned. You just *know* how far to sit it in. You'll get the ratio in no time (maybe after a few disasters!). This is our first introduction to the 'Goldilocks Rule'… the perfect place is *always* somewhere in between. If the stone is sitting too deep and there is too much metal, it will be a nightmare to push over, which will end up looking a mess.

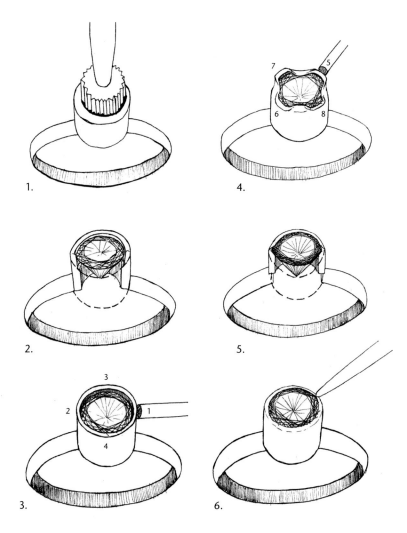

Bezel setting technique. (Jennifer Colquhoun)

Whereas if the stone is too shallow with just a sliver of metal, you run the risk of the stone falling out.

Step 5

Time to set. Make sure you're sitting correctly and have mimicked the basic technique we've previously discussed. At the four compass points, carefully push over the side of the metal towards the stone. This should be a 'rock and roll' motion. Don't push too hard and fold the metal in too far. We want to carefully blend the metal over. If we warp it immediately, it is incredibly difficult to keep it nice and round. Your push tool should be half on the wall, half peeking over.

Step 6

Now do the same at the four points in between your original push points. Make sure the stone is straight at all times and not flipping up. This indicates you've pushed too hard at one point. This *can* be rectified, but it involves nudging the wall back up with a scorper. This greatly increases the risk of a stone chipping. Prevention is the best form of cure!

Step 7

Repeat the process again for all the places that haven't been pushed over yet. Always try to keep the wall of the setting smooth and even. Remember to use your core and full arm for this. 'Wristing' it will do nothing but frustrate you. Use your loupe and check the metal is moving. You'll eventually be able to see where you've pushed without the need for a loupe or optivisors.

Step 8

Keep pushing the edge towards the stone, overlapping where you are pushing again and again and again. This ensures the edge is kept even, rather than angular. It is this 'blending' technique that keeps both the outer and inner edges smooth and without dips or wobbly sections. If you see a section that looks out of place, work on it gently until it has been nudged into where it should be. Remember to constantly check if the stone is straight from all angles and if it is solidly in place.

Step 9

When you are satisfied that the edge is fully over, smooth and even with no gaps between wall and stone, carefully burnish the inside edge to give a bright cut finish. When doing this, a slender burnisher with a narrow tip is best. Don't drag your burnisher across the stone. You

HINTS AND TIPS

- Sometimes we can burr in a slightly squint fashion. To counter this, constantly turn your job around in the ring clamp or dop stick. The slight bias will then be corrected as you burr from all angles.
- To check that your stone is straight, put your finger directly above the setting. The shadow makes it easier to see how the stone sits.
- If you're having trouble pushing the edge over, file a little away on the outer wall to make it slightly thinner.
- You will naturally be tempted to push right at the top of the edge. If you are struggling, push further down behind the edge.
- Do *not* polish the end of your push tool. I've seen methods that insist on this. While I understand the reasons (to prevent bruising on the wall), this will only increase your risk of slipping and causing serious injury. The tool must be *lightly* textured to give grip, but not mark where you are pushing. If you do have a deep score or scratch, we can gently remove it with a light needle file, then finish as normal.

Bezel set ring. Crisp, precise and in perfect proportions, this mixed metal bezel set ring has been created by Marc Lange to give maximum effect. (Marc Lange)

Step 10

Now file the outer edge gently until it is crisp and sharp. Your push tool should have created a natural 45-degree angle over the edge of the stone. Use a needle file to accentuate this look, but stay well away from the top of the stone. At the same time, please do not file too much of the wall away... cardinal sin! If you do this you'll be kicking yourself for a week! Use emery or silicones to tidy up any file marks.

Summary

A well-executed bezel setting is a true thing of beauty. There's just something about that clean precision, alongside that narrow halo of metal that either complements or clashes with the gemstone. Safe, secure and simple, bezel setting is definitely one of your starting points on your jewellery journey.

are dicing with death! The burnisher can score, scrape or chip a stone, particularly a vulnerable one. You will most definitely learn this as you go along. It's a funny method that requires you to apply force to achieve a bright finish, but at the same time avoid the stone. Again, we are working in very fine margins (best get used to this!).

Claw Setting

The most simple form of setting and the most widely used. Claw setting is used to let everyone see the beautiful gemstone, due to the

A lesson on how to perfectly create beautiful clusters. Each stone is expertly set and held in by a variety of claws. It looks simple, but is far from it! (Ryan Nelson)

limited amount of metal it needs. Also known as prong setting, it is clean, classic and contemporary, and accounts for the vast majority of stone set jewellery. Similarly to bezel, most claw setting requires burring away the metal to seat the stone before setting. Sometimes a 'gallery' is used as a seat to give extra pressure displacement, other times the stone simply 'floats' within the claws. This requires a little bit more attention due to the fragile and precarious nature of the setting. Yes, claw settings show off the stone in all its glory, but a near-naked stone can be a vulnerable one.

We have to pay particular attention to the pressure on the stone. If it is being held in by four claws, then there is a great deal of pressure concentrated at these four points on what can be a soft stone. In that respect, we have to ensure the stone sits on a nice, comfortable seat that will displace the pressure evenly around it. If it doesn't have a seat, the setter must make sure the claw is thick and deep enough to make a good notch in there so the stone slots in, and set with craft and thought.

Theory

In principle, claw setting is relatively simple. Bend some prongs over the stone and you're laughing. However, while it's probably the easiest to master, getting it right to begin with can prove tricky. A poorly seated stone may end up wobbling around. A hefty push of a claw can end up flipping a stone miles out of place. Trimming the claws back after setting can also prove dangerous. It can look easy, but as with all stone setting, there's a lot more involved than meets the eye.

Sometimes simplicity is the best. This single-stone solitaire engagement ring was made with a 1.07ct diamond and set with elegant, short talon-style claws. No fuss, just bling! (Vanilla Ink)

Before you start

Take a moment to assess the task in hand. Think about where you will be cutting the metal away, how the prong will fold over the gem, what length and finish the claw will be. A poorly set or finished claw mount can drastically alter not only the look of the piece but its durability or life expectancy too.

Different techniques

Seated on a gallery or bearer wire

As the title suggests, this method is where the stone sits snugly upon a little seat. This ensures that the pressure on the stone from the claws is displaced evenly around the pavilion, just underneath the girdle. This can be in single or double gallery form. Ideally, the seat is not visible from the top of the stone; preferably it tucks in underneath the girdle and is just shy of the outside measurement. During the manufacture of the setting, a notch will be filed into the outside of the seat (and bottom if making a double gallery). Not only does this give the claw somewhere to locate into when soldering,

Baroque Jewellery – Black diamond ring. An excellent side profile shot to show how a stone should sit in the setting. Note the perfect proportions and the ideal amount of claw set over the stone. (James Morris)

but it means that each claw will need a section burred away to ensure the stone sits in place. This means the claws will be tight against the stone, hugging it nice and close as opposed to having a gap. Fresh air between claw and stone is a big no-no.

Method

Step 1
As with bezel setting, make sure your job is securely held. While we don't often need to push quite as hard for claws, an error can be incredibly painful. Ask any setter who has been unfortunate enough to slip, wedging a nice, sharp claw right up their fingernail. Ouch.

Step 2
Take the appropriate size of burr that matches your stone size. Use a 5mm burr for a 5mm stone and so on. Use your pliers and bend out the claws ever so slightly (this isn't applicable for tapered settings), making sure you're not bruising the claws too much. Ideally, the stone *should not* sit on its seat without burring down. The action of cutting the metal away not only helps the claw to be pushed over the stone but if we burr away just enough and no more to sit the stone, it should receive a nice, tight hug from each claw.

Step 3
Once you have burred down, sit your stone in place, checking carefully to see if it sits neatly on its seat and each claw has a notch out for the girdle to sit in. I repeat; the stone has to be on its seat. That's the whole purpose of this method. There is no point creating a nice seat, only for the stone to hover above it like it's using a public lavatory. The stone should also be good and tight, not rocking around. If it's too loose, it'll slip all over the place when setting. It'll be like trying to climb a greasy pole. Nobody wants that.

Step 4
Start by slightly pushing one claw over, then

the opposite one. Repeat the process with the remaining two. Keep this up until the claws are completely pushed over onto the stone. All the time, check that the stone is straight and hasn't flipped slightly. Also, have a good look to see that the claws have bent at a nice angle to the stone, rather than curling over with fresh air underneath. This can often happen with thicker claws that require more effort to push over.

Step 5

Now it's time to decide how you want the claws to look. Short and round, or long and slender like a talon? Very carefully, saw the claws back to the desired size. You'll need a thin saw blade for this. The idea here is not to cut the excess off entirely, but stop just shy and kind of flick the rest off when it's hanging by a thread. The majority of gemstones do not enjoy having the sharp teeth of a blade dragged across them.

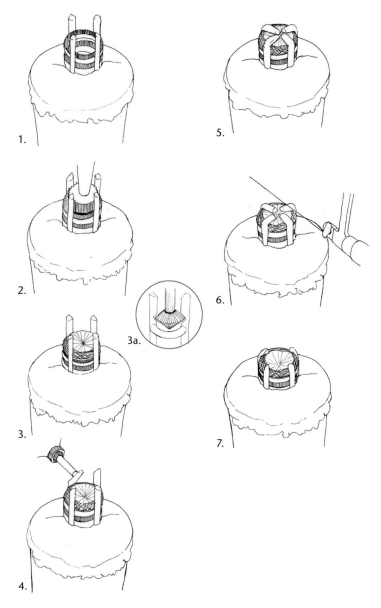

1.

2.

3a.

3.

4.

5.

6.

7.

Claw setting
technique.
(Jennifer
Colquhoun)

Yellow gold emerald claw set ring. Something a little different from William White. The elongated talon-style claws work beautifully to hold the rich cabochon emerald in place. (William White)

Step 6

Take a safety-back needle file and neatly finish the claws. All the time, *do not* drag the file across the stone. You're looking to be intelligent here, using deft strokes to shape your claw while being conscious of the delicate nature of the gem. Yes, diamonds will be fine here, but if you teach yourself to respect all stones, your technique will be the same, no matter what you are setting. If you have decided to finish your claw in the more traditional sense, roll the file over the cut claw to create an even, rounded ball. For finishing it like a talon, taper it gently to a point, still being careful to round it slightly for comfort. Just make sure that there is no flash metal or sharp edges that can snag on loose clothing. Even if a claw is finished with flat edges (more common with shaped stones but sometimes seen on rounds too), it still needs to be smooth, polished and not something that can cause injury.

Set without a seat or into claws only

With this style, our stone has no seat to sit on at all. The claws are taking all the pressure here, with great care needed to ensure safety and longevity. Sometimes the setting can be a tight taper, naturally allowing the stone to sit into it, with only a small amount required to cut away for gem location. At other times, a far

Trio of claw set rings. A masterclass by Stefanie Verhoef in how to use oversize claws to set stones and as a strong feature. Note how the stone sits snugly within the claws, protected and safe from any knocks or bashes the ring may take. (Josephine Verhoef/Lieke van Kalken)

beefier, more sturdy claw is required, meaning precision seating with either a setting burr or bearing cutter is needed. With this method, the claw cannot be slender or weak. They need to serve their purpose of providing robust protection and even displacement of pressure. An insipid claw can result in the stone coming loose, falling out or becoming damaged over time. However, set correctly, the effect can look incredible.

Method

Step 1

Okay, so we have no seat, only claws. We have to create somewhere for the stones to sit by using burrs, just like some rascal has taken a sneaky bite out of a cake. This can be done with either a setting burr or a bearing cutter. Biting is not recommended. We have to study the shape of the stone in relation to the claw. Think about what kind of angle needs to be burred away for the stone to slot in nicely. Also, are the claws going to be folded over, or are we attempting just to slide the stone into place and give the claws a gentle squeeze for security?

Step 2

If we are going to fold the claws over, similar to the previous method, a setting burr should do the trick. Again, your stone should not sit in the correct place without creating a seat. If your setting is straight up and down, nudge the claws out a tad like before; if it is tapered, then the claws are already wide open and ready to accept the stone. Gently burr down as before, although this time, we have no seat to let us know when we've reached the ideal point. This can be dangerous, as many a stone has been sat too deep due to over-zealous burr work. Take your time, making sure you are constantly checking how the stone sits. Fold over the claws as before, making sure it isn't flipping around or sitting squint.

Step 3

Our other option is to use a bearing cutter to create a lovely negative image of the stone's shape. Look closely at the angles required and mimic them perfectly. Not only do they have to be the exact same shape, but they have to sit at the correct height too. Begin by positioning the stone in the claws and imagining where you want it to sit. You can even mark on where you should burr on all claws if you wish. For this style, we're also applying the Goldilocks Rule. If we burr too much away, there will be horrible gaps left with light poking through. This is never pretty. Or, worst-case scenario, you burr far too much away, resulting in a weak claw that may fall off. However, if we don't take enough metal away, the stone will not be held in by much at all. This will leave it unsteady, unsafe and oh-so vulnerable.

Step 4

Now, on to finishing. There isn't much more to be said here that we haven't already discussed in the previous method. If done correctly, your

HINTS AND TIPS

- If it is possible, it's often a good idea to remove your job from the ring clamp or setter's wax to view the complete piece. Every now and then, a stone can look straight in a clamp, but it's actually a tad off.
- Always leave the claw longer before you set. Don't be tempted to trim right back before pushing. A longer claw is a simpler one to ease over the stone. Just remember you don't need to leave them like flagpoles.
- To check if your claws are smooth and won't snag, rub the finished job up and down your clothes. If the claws collect threads and fibres, back to the bench for you.
- Some setters like to finish with a cup burr or similar, but I'm always wary of going near fragile gemstones with something that can be quite devastating to them. I just use a trusty safety-back needle file and maybe emery sticks or silicones if I dare. I find that most claws will polish up nicely from here if you take care and use precision when you go to do the final polish.

'Atlantis' ring. Yet another stunning piece of work from Baroque Jewellery. The whole ring is a true work of art, with the main centre stone being held in by elegant, slender talon style claws. (James Morris)

stone should sit just as solid as if it was on a gallery or seat. If folding the claws completely over, finish them in the same manner. However, if leaving the claws protruding, take a little time to check they don't snag or catch on things. An oversized, beefy claw can look incredible; just make sure you aren't manufacturing a weapon that will have someone's eye out in a flash!

Summary

With more options available for overall looks and finishes, claw setting can be explored in great depth once the basics have been mastered. Experiments can be performed with claw length and look, as well as setting styles and shapes. Don't forget that once you become quite proficient, settings and claws can also be adorned with stones too, making complex but striking pieces of jewellery.

'Fluted' ring. Baroque Jewellery's elegant 'Fluted' ring shows how to execute 'talon'-style claws perfectly. The elongated rose gold complements the brown diamond perfectly, combining to create a stunning effect. (James Morris)

FLUSH AND TENSION SETTING

Flush Setting

Flush setting is very similar in principle to bezel setting, in that the edge of the metal is pushed over and finished crisply on the inside edge. Only this time, there's no wall to deal with as the stone sits snugly within the metal.

I have seen many different ways to flush set in my time, with some of them being shockingly precarious, as only a tiny amount of metal is used to hold the stone in place. Similarly, I know of some setters who like to 'click' the stone into place. However, there is no way I am going to adopt that technique, nor am I going to teach it. I do not want to rely on sheer luck for a peridot, emerald or tanzanite to click in there.

Such delicate stones require more finesse and care, with a safer, more dexterous method required. I also do not like simply burnishing the metal over the stone once seated, as I would much prefer my setting was rock solid and secure within my jewellery. This may prove to be a controversial opinion, or cause much tutting from my fellow setters, but I strongly believe we should be ensuring the stones are solidly in place while giving ourselves the best chance of achieving a professional finish.

Theory

Flush setting requires the edge to be pushed down over the stone before any burnishing takes place. This means the setting is far safer. A push tool (much smaller and more delicate than your claw or bezel pusher) is used to 'pinch' the edge of the metal down over the stone, smoothing it over time, before finishing with a burnisher to create a crisp, bright inside edge. This extra method, which was taught to me as an apprentice, allows for extra security and a cleaner inside edge.

The absolute key to this style of setting is keeping the hole as tight as possible. A stone that wobbles about in a flush setting seat is one that is unlikely to be set.

LEFT: **Vanilla Ink – 'Green-eyed Monster'. True opulence and extravagance, this one-off beauty from Vanilla Ink strays from the traditional and offers a contemporary way to tension set a stone. (Vanilla Ink)**

Korus Design – 'Bubbles' ring. A perfect blend of scattered flush setting using a variety of stone colours and sizes, finished off perfectly with a brushed effect. (Vesa Peltonen)

A signature style 'Button' ring from William White, using a centre stone complemented with smaller accent stones, all flush set to perfection. (William White)

Before you start

When judging flush setting, you have to account for a number of factors. Is your surface flat, court or 'D' section? Each one will require individual thought. Setting into a flat surface is lovely and straightforward, as burr-ing to a consistent depth is relatively simple. However, when setting into a 'D' section, we must account for the curve. This cross-section should help:

As we can see, that sweet little 'happy medium' must be found (we need to find that a lot in stone setting – not too deep, not too

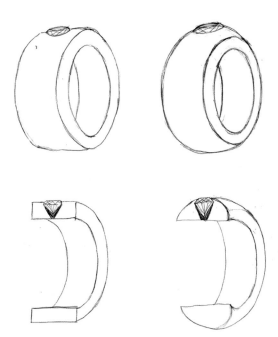

'D' section vs flat flush setting cross-section. (Jennifer Colquhoun)

OPENING UP HOLES

This is relevant for flush, pavé, channel and microclaw, we simply *must* be aware of drilling through and opening up holes. This is what we mean when we discuss 'an appropriate size'. On most (but not all) occasions, the job will require to be drilled all the way through. But to what size? Is there a formula, a magic number to follow? Unfortunately not, is the answer. We have to use our intelligence and skill to figure this out. My method of opening up and cleaning out the hole may not be everyone's method, but I'm hoping it makes sense to you.

First of all, *do not* make the depth of your job *less* than the depth of the stone. This makes me angry. Now, we consider opening up our holes to a good size that's in proportion to the overall dimensions of the metal. If you take away too much, you will compromise the integrity of the structure of the piece, making it weak. I've messed up several times in this way, removing too much metal, then when I've gone to set, the damn job simply collapsed on me as it wasn't strong enough to handle all the pushing. And the thing is, there's no way back from that, the job is ruined and must be started again.

I reckon it would help if I gave an example. Let's say we're setting a 3mm stone into a 5mm flat band. This is bread and butter stuff. We will go into more detail in the following method, but here's what I would do. Start by drilling all the way through with a 1mm drill, then open up with either larger drills or ball burrs. I prefer to use ball burrs, as I feel they give more control when removing metal. For a 3mm stone in a 5mm ring, I would open up *all the way through* up to 2mm. This gives plenty of metal in the ring for strength and durability. Now I would burr three-quarters of the way down with a 2.5mm burr. This removes a lot of the metal from underneath where the stones sit. The reason I do this is that the more metal the stone sits on, the more chance it has of moving around. I believe that there should be plenty of space for the stone to sit in, and not interfering with the bottom of it. The other reason for this is to give your burrs less work to do. If we drilled through with a 1mm drill, then went straight in with a 3mm setting burr to open up, not only would we be there for ages, but you're giving your burr far too difficult a job to do, therefore putting unnecessary stress onto it, and reducing its lifespan. These tools can be expensive, look after them! Now that you've done all the preparation, you can go ahead and seat your stone.

Pair of flush set rings. A beautiful pair of sapphires are set crisp and sharp within both 18ct red and white gold versions of Oxx Jewellery's rings. (Juliet Sheath)

shallow – it's the Goldilocks Rule!). If we plunge the stone in too far, we'll never get the meatiest part of the metal over. However, not burring down enough will leave the edges of the stone exposed. While this can sometimes look pretty as a feature, most of the time we would like them firmly set in the metal, thank you very much. Court shape, or just slightly rounded, poses similar problems, just not as extreme. Do you think this is complicated? Wait until you hit the later chapters!

Method

Step 1
Mark where you want your stone to sit with a centre punch (or similar). You can take a small hand drill and create a 'pilot' hole if you want (I always find this useful and still use this method when drilling). Now use your pendant motor with a 1mm drill and go all the way through. If you're old school and wish to drill without a pendant motor, good luck and look after those blisters!

Step 2
Continue to open out the hole to an appropriate size. Use steadily increasing ball burrs to do this. Each job will be different. It will be a proportionate ratio between the metal and stone. If you have to drill all the way through, be aware of the structure of the metal. It still has to be strong. However, we cut away the metal underneath to give the stone the best chance of sitting down cleanly, so you have to find a balance. Too much metal in the hole makes the burr work harder, shortening its life and increasing the time taken. However, too little and you run the risk of the stone falling through or your job collapsing. Be aware (*see box above*).

Step 3
Once you're happy, take a setting burr (3mm for a 3mm stone and so on) and gently cut a seat for the stone. Go steadily. You want the table of the stone to be approximately flush with the surface of the metal. Seat your stone. Make sure it is straight. Place the flat of the push tool on the lip of the hole, slightly leaning towards the stone. Push down and rock your wrist to rub over the edge of the metal. It should create a 45-degree angle. It's almost a pinch of the metal, leaning in towards the stone. It should be clean and smooth. If you lean to one side or the other, you will end up 'chewing' the metal, which looks awful. Once you get this right, you will only get better. Repeat the process directly opposite to where you've just worked, then at the other compass points.

Step 4
Similarly to bezel setting, do the same at the four points in between. Make sure the stone is straight at all times. Repeat the process again for all the places that haven't been pushed over yet. Always try to keep the inside edge of the setting even.

Step 5
Keep pushing the edge down towards the stone, overlapping where you are pushing again and again and again. This ensures it is kept smooth and consistent. The constant overlapping flattens down the edge and blends in any marks. Don't dig in with the push tool. This creates ridges in the setting that prove difficult to fix.

Step 6
Now go over the top of the stone, to the opposite side of the stone we've been working on so far, and use your push tool as a burnisher. You want to sweep it gently from side to side, making sure you keep the tool away from the stone. This is tricky. Dragging metal along a soft stone can chip or crack it.

Step 7
Once you're happy, take your burnisher and go into the edge from the original side again, just like when you pushed initially. Use the sweeping motion once more to bright cut the inner edge. Again, be careful of the stone.

**Flush setting
step by step.
(Jennifer
Colquhoun)**

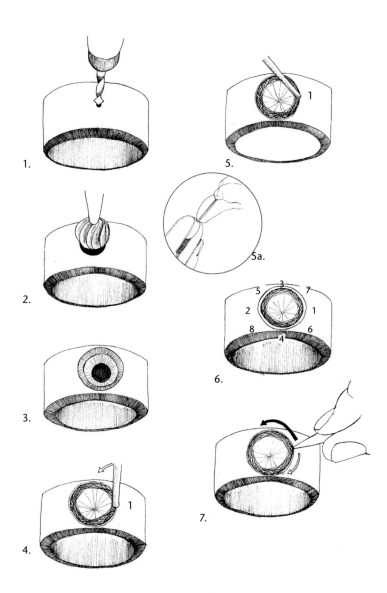

TIPS FOR FLUSH SETTING

- Practise with your push tool before you start. Create lines of the nice half-crescent shape that the push tool should make. It's the most important part.
- Take care when drilling through the metal. Multiple settings that have been 'opened up' too much can weaken a piece of jewellery.
- The girdle of the stone has to be below the edge of the metal. It cannot be set otherwise.

A range of red, white and yellow 'Us' rings by Korus of Finland, using flush setting to maximum effect. (Teemu Töyrylä)

Summary

Flush setting can appear easy, however, there's a lot more to it than meets the eye. The technique requires a finish which is simplistic, crisp and without fuss. It gives the impression of an 'entry level' technique, but now that you've had a go, you'll understand why we class it as 'intermediate'. As previously discussed, my method takes us above and beyond most setters' paths, but I genuinely encourage you to adopt this way. I think it is safer and allows you to create a lovely clean finish around the stone, which enhances the look and gives a pleasing end result.

Set with over forty diamonds, Vanilla Ink's 'Aero' ring gives the effect of bubbles flowing along unique and angular shapes. (Stacey Bentley)

TENSION SETTING

In stark contrast to most of the stone setting techniques, tension setting is the new kid on the block. Developed in the late 1960s by German pioneers Niessing, the style has a magical feel to it, due to the stone appearing to 'float' in the air.

It's not a method that I've used a great deal during my career; the demand for it seems to be few and far between. This may be down to the fact that it really is difficult to master. Many, many a stone has gone bye-bye from a poorly manufactured tension set piece. A ring that can be prized apart with little or no effort is not tension setting and will end in disaster for you and the client. Great care must be given to executing the method with correct dimensions and accurate burring.

Dutch designer Marc Lange uses mixed metals and various setting styles to perfection, with the star of the show being the perfectly tension set diamond. (Mark Lange)

Theory

The actual name of this style is somewhat misleading, due to the fact that it is *pressure* that holds the stone in, rather than *tension*. But whatever, let's just get on with it. Tension setting sounds far sexier, anyway. Strict rules must be followed when it comes to getting this right. The correct dimensions of metal must be used. There is no magic formula when it

Etched rose cut diamond ring. The wonderful etched effect on this ring complements the rose cut salt and pepper diamond in the most dramatic way. (Peter W. Gilroy)

Single stone tension set ring. Lithuania-based jeweller Asr Jwls uses unique metal alloys to create unusual yet stunning diamond set rings. (Augusta Sofija Rudzikaite)

comes to this, rather a good knowledge and some experience of metalwork and the physics involved. Beefy, sturdy metal must be used as well as your chosen alloy either being naturally hard or work-hardened before setting. It's this stiffness that allows the stone to be held in for, well, pretty much forever! Accurate burring and seating the stone is the final ingredient to this setting stew. Too much and it'll rock around, too little and it'll fall out.

Before you start

Whatever you do, the piece you are setting into must be strong enough, so that it is impossible to prize apart without tools. That's it, plain and simple. I've seen pieces that were 'tension set' that looked like the stone would fall out if the wind changed direction. Technically, they have indeed executed tension setting, but if the ring was too thin, it isn't going to last long. A solid metal must be used, or alternatively, the dimen-

sions of the piece are oversized or extremely work-hardened to ensure no natural movement can happen. Finally, make sure you're using a crisp, sharp burr. There isn't much margin for error, here. Give yourself the best chance to begin with.

Method

Step 1
Okay, we have made sure the metal we're working with is of a heavy gauge and/or a hard alloy. That bad boy ain't moving anywhere. If this is a ring, can we *please* ensure that the point of the stone does not sit lower than the inside of the ring? It's a *huge* pet hate of mine. I don't understand why you would manufacture a ring, only for the hard, scratchy culet of the stone to be sitting on the client's finger! Just please don't, okay? Before you begin making the piece, measure your stone and build the mount so it can take the depth of the stone.

Tension setting technique. (Jennifer Colquhoun)

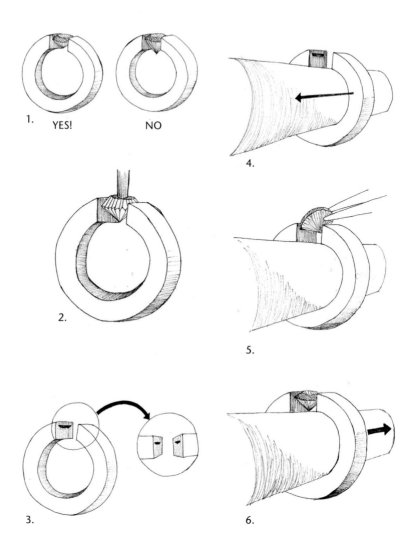

1. YES! NO

2.

3.

4.

5.

6.

Step 2

We're ready to go. Measure the stone that you will be setting and make sure that the gap between the ends of the metal is lesser than the stone itself. However, to allow the burr in to cut the seat, this may have to be opened up, then readjusted before finally sitting the stone in place.

Step 3

We're going to be using a setting burr. These follow the shape of (most) stones pretty accurately. Please make sure you do this intelligently, and precisely. A slip with a burr can set you back a few steps, so be careful. Take a look at the shape of the stone. We need to mimic that in negative form *perfectly*, so that the stone slots in beautifully with no movement either up or down, or side to side.

Step 4

Burr smoothly and evenly on either side of the gap, making sure you're going to the same depth on both faces, as well as burring at the same level. So many stones have been set crooked due to these inaccuracies. You thought

Stack of tension set rings. Peter Gilroy's etched rings in various metals are a true work of art. The wide, detailed ring shanks enhance the look of the sharply set diamonds. (Peter W. Gilroy)

this looked easy, didn't you? Well, you need to be mindful that the seat you're cutting is also deadly straight and not tilting down to one side, either. With so many factors requiring such precision, you can now see why so many tension set pieces have either failed or never seen the outside world.

Step 5

It's funny because in theory, tension setting seems simple. Burr a seat, slot the stone in... ta da! But anyone who has ever attempted or mastered the method will tell you how tricky it can be. Now that we've burred away our seat (which of course is perfect), it's time to actually set the stone. Take the time to be sure that the gap in the piece is correct. It's Goldilocks time. If it is spaced too far apart, well, your stone is just going to fall out, isn't it? Too close, and you're running the risk of damaging the stone. Tension setting is a great way to protect softer stones, but too much pressure when setting can stress that delicate wee thing so much that it can't take it and shatters. Be warned!

Step 6

We have to prise the ring open to allow the stone in. But again, be careful. If we open it up too much, it'll lose the desired tension in the ring. We must open it gently to allow the stone in and no more. I like to do this on my mandrel, holding it almost vertical, resting on the 'V' of my bench peg while I slide the ring on. If I balance the handle of the mandrel on my chest, it frees up both hands to slot the stone in place. This can be incredibly tricky, as we have to open the ring up by only a fraction to allow for the dimensions of the stone. Many a stone has been lost or bounced about all over the bench, refusing to slide into its new home. Use sticky tack, tweezers, or whatever you feel

TIPS FOR TENSION SETTING

- Tension setting cannot be sized. Always check with your client (then double check) before committing to stone setting.
- Study the shape and dimensions of the stone you are setting. Copy them exactly, creating a perfect negative for the stone to slot into.
- When choosing stones, avoid thick girdles like the plague. A poorly cut stone is incredibly difficult to set.
- Make sure that the face of your ring where you have burred away is polished and finished just before setting. You won't get into it to clean up once it's in place.

most comfortable with to help the stone slip in. Once it's located and in place, slowly push the ring back down the mandrel, watching the stone like a hawk the entire time. Hopefully, it sits deadly straight all ways and is rock solid. Well done!

Summary

Tension setting is probably the cleanest, most clinical-looking way of setting stones. Again, like so many others, it can look simple, yet effective. But you and I both know just how complex it can be, yearning for prior thought, and screaming out for precision. A well-executed tension set ring truly is a thing of beauty to behold, basic in looks, but hiding a great deal of technical, methodical processes. The jewellery world most definitely thanks the genius of Neissing for their creation.

PAVÉ SETTING

Pavé is by far and away my favourite form of setting. There's just something about the crisp, clean process that gives me enormous satisfaction. I've adapted my method as I've travelled along my jewellery journey, making sure I now clean out the metal first, rather than 'raising the grain', then cutting away metal.

Older textbooks will show you this technique, which is one I used for nearly fifteen years before a real 'Eureka!' moment showed me the best way. I was never happy with the end results of pavé; I always felt there was too much metal around the stones, which gave the overall job an untidy and clumsy look. I kept seeing other setters' work and wondered how they managed to achieve such crisp results before it hit me on the head like a sledgehammer! With a few tweaks here and there, I've finely honed it to an economical and logical technique.

I now look back on previous pavé and cringe a little, desperate to get my hands on the job and do it the right way! I have seen many variations of cutting away metal first; as my method is entirely self-taught, it may be a little unique. But I enjoy the control and the clean, bright results it gives.

Theory

Pavé setting takes its name from the French for 'paved surface'. Often known as bead set or grain set, it is the art of setting stones using tiny bits of metal, which are then polished and rounded to become shiny, before cutting a bright cut border around. It is insanely tricky to master. Yes, you may understand the theory and set the stones, but it's the refinement of these skills that truly matters.

An uneven bright cut, or out of place bead, or beads that are irregular in size immediately leap out at the client and grab their attention. While

LEFT: **Pavé setting is often used as a flourish to allow a centre stone to feel more alive, but in this case we added beautiful sapphires to the side of the wedding ring so they would dance and sing from a different angle. (Vanilla Ink)**

18ct yellow gold diamond loop ring. The elegant loops and dramatic curves of McCaul Goldsmith beautiful diamond earrings display a masterclass in how to use single row pavé to accentuate a design. (Keith Leighton)

Sugar skull ring. Probably one of the most enjoyable commissions we've had at Vanilla Ink, Pete's sugar skull ring had one eye to represent his optically-challenged pet cat. The diamond was delicately pavé set with five beads. Such an amazing piece of jewellery. (Vanilla Ink)

they may not entirely understand why their job looks off, if military-style uniform and spacing is not met, it will always appear wrong.

Time must be taken to refine, refine and refine those skills. Make your beads smaller, cut your lines straighter, make your gravers sharper, be braver with removing metal. This will all come in time, but you'll have the most fun trying to master this amazing technique.

TECHNIQUES

We run a full day session on learning how to pavé set. In the morning, we teach 'single row' pavé, which introduces the basic technique required and allows the students to practise cutting their clean lines. At this point, we also introduce the difference between 'splitting' the bead and 'sharing' the bead. There is no right or wrong when it comes to this. However, as single row pavé can be curved as well as on a straight line, sometimes physics dictates and

automatically selects for you. While splitting the bead can maybe prove to be a tad more secure, the downside is that it can be trickier due to the smaller scale of the beads required. One slip and it's gone! Sharing the bead comes with its own pitfalls, as the stones must be as close together as possible to ensure each bead holds two stones in. The upside is that it can give an overall cleaner, less busy finish to the job. Choose your technique wisely!

Before you start

Pavé requires accuracy. The aim is to get the stones as tight together as possible without touching each other. If they are too far away from one another, not only can it look clumsy, but you may struggle to set them. Pavé requires a great deal of patience and a whole lot of preparation. If you can accept this before you begin, it'll help you to learn. When drilling and burring for each stone, I like to do each one individually, rather than committing to drilling all holes through first. While this may take a *little* longer,

I feel it gives me control over the placement of each hole. If I have measured incorrectly, or drilled inaccurately, I can adjust as I go along. If you commit to drilling all holes before burring, a mistake can ruin a job. Remember to burr out enough metal beneath the stones (*see* Flush Setting chapter). The more metal the stone sits on, the more chance it has of wobbling around. And as we discussed in the previous chapter, it's all about conserving your burrs as well. Don't make them work harder than they need to. Finally, please make sure that all your scorpers are sharp. Not only will it make cutting easier, but it will also reduce the risk of damage to the job, the stones or yourself.

Single row pavé

Method

Step 1
Use dividers to mark a straight line in the centre of the metal to create a guideline. Figure out where your first stone will go and mark it out. Drill down and burr out the hole to an appropriate size. For how to do this, please see the box before the flush setting method in Chapter 3.

Step 2
Take a setting burr (3mm for a 3mm stone and so on) and gently cut a seat for each stone. Make sure you always use a lube of some sort (we just use good old 3-in-1 oil). You want the table of the stone to sit approximately just above the surface of the metal. Repeat these actions until you have all seats cut. Remember to clean out the previous seat with a burr or a soft toothbrush as you go along and check your stones are sitting evenly.

Step 3
Using dividers or a scorper, lightly score or mark a line a fraction outside the lip of the holes. This creates a 'frame', which helps you to under-stand where you'll be cutting. (It isn't necessary to do this, but I always think it helps me keep my cutting even. I'm forever encouraging students to implement techniques to make life easy for themselves, something which should remain with you throughout your career.)

Step 4
Take an appropriate, sharp flat scorper. This will relate to the size of your stone (*see* diagram). From the line you've marked, cut the metal away from the sides at a 45-degree angle. The sharp nose of the scorper should lodge into the line you created. This helps to cut. The aim is to leave metal in between for the beads. Refine your cutting until you're happy with the bead size. In an ideal world, we cut with one smooth motion, but until you nail the technique, multiple cuts are fine. Sometimes we don't have the perfect size of scorper either, so will be forced to cut a few times. Just make sure you do them all at the same angle.

Step 5
Use a cross-cut burr, ball burr or scorper to cut out the metal between each stone seat. Make sure it's bright cut and clean. All that's left now should be your beads. It's at this point you decide whether to split or share the beads. Either way is acceptable, but if your job is on a curve, the bead position should naturally appear to you.

Step 6
Burr any flash away to clean out the seats. Sit the stones down, table flush with the surface of the metal.

Step 7
Use your sharp scorper to nudge the beads over. You want to drive a wedge down between the metal, then roll it over or between the stones. Keep alternating where you are pushing to ensure your stone stays straight. Make sure the beads are firmly down and the stone is rock solid. Move to the next stone and repeat. (With a shared bead, you want to push the bead in between both stones as far as possible. This

helps the metal to lock both stones at once. When splitting the bead, you have to initially drive the metal forwards before turning 90 degrees to splay the metal outwards and over each of the stones.)

Step 8

Take an appropriately sized beader and gently rock in a circular motion to create a bead over the stone. The concave shape of the beader smoothes the metal over to create a shiny, rounded bead. Be careful to use the right size.

Too large and you run the risk of chipping stones, too small and you'll create a 'fried egg' effect!

Step 9

Use scorpers to clean behind the beads, making the corners nice and crisp. There should be enough room to get a graver or spitzstick behind the beads. If the scorper is cutting away the bead, it isn't over enough. Go along the straight edge with a sharp scorper to create a clean, bright cut. Remember that the face of

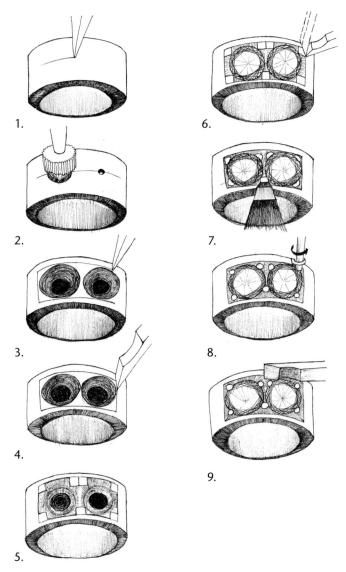

1.

2.

3.

4.

5.

6.

7.

8.

9.

Pavé setting step by step. (Jennifer Colquhoun)

TIPS FOR SINGLE ROW PAVÉ

- You will always need to take away more metal than you think. Be brave!
- Try to cut with one firm motion. This makes it look clean and crisp.
- Scribe or mark where your beads will be. This will help you to see how much metal to cut away.
- Use a smaller scorper when splitting the bead so as not to chip stones.

the scorper will transfer whatever finish it has onto the metal. Take the time to high polish your finishing scorper. The end result should have straight lines, crisp corners, even-size beads (all in a row) and stones set all on the same level. The finishing process should be easy due to your prior preparation. Don't tinker too much or you can remove a bead or cut through the outer walls.

Multiple Pavé

This relates to any form of pavé setting that isn't simply in a single row. It can be structured, it can be in a grid, it can be staggered – it can be anything! And again, I completely adore doing it. I thoroughly enjoy the meticulous process of cutting out metal between each stone, and the alarming danger of not knocking a vital bead away. Some may say it's daunting; I just like the thrill of it all!

A classic style of ring from Korus, with the stunning centre stone being complemented by the pavé set shoulders. Note the nice extra touch of millgrain detail. (Vesa Peltonen)

Grid vs staggered pavé setting. The various choices that multiple pavé will throw at you. Each style, whether it be grid, staggered or random, offers a variety of methods for cutting beads. Remember, as long as it looks deliberate, it will be acceptable. Sometimes there is no right or wrong; instead, it comes down to personal preference. (Jennifer Colquhoun)

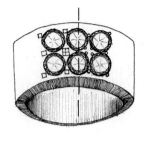

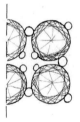

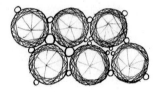

Theory

The principle is the same as the previous method. I always teach that each stage of pavé setting automatically leads to the next. You measure, drill the hole, cut the metal to slide away until you are left with your beads to then set with. Keep on practising until you master it. But throw in the chaos of stones right next to each other on all sides, then that lovely, rigid structure of what to cut and when flies out the window!

The aim of the game is to take away metal from where the stones nearly touch each other, not the metal in *between* them all. This is the most vital part as the metal left behind becomes the keystone to holding two or three stones in place. The more you do this, the more it makes sense. You'll eventually see everything clearly, maybe even before you've burred a seat away. Experience comes with time and rewards you greatly.

For this tutorial, we're going to look at staggering the stones. But once you understand this and have attempted a few goes, the technique crosses over to grid and random.

Method

Step 1
Mark, drill and burr out your stones exactly the same way as you did for the single row. Now we are going to add another row of three underneath, but staggered rather than grid.

Step 2
The first stone in the second row slots nicely in between stone one and two of the first row. The second row then carries on in the usual pattern. Drill, burr and seat the second row.

Step 3
Using a scorper or dividers, lightly score or mark a line a fraction outside the lip of the holes. At the same time, scribe or mark on where your beads will be. This will help you to see how much metal to cut away and from where. (It's worth taking the time to do this. Even now I can still get a bit mixed up where I'm cutting away. Make life easy for yourself and mark a dot on with a fine marker pen to show you where your beads will be.)

Murazzo – Grid/staggered pavé rings. Two brilliant examples of how to make the different styles of multiple pavé work. Each is a triple row of diamonds; however, the two styles give an entirely different look to the trained eye. Michael Muratore executes each style flawlessly. (Michael Muratore)

TIPS FOR MULTIPLE PAVÉ

- Your scorper must remain sharp. A blunt tool can cause serious injury.
- You can use a marker pen for multiple pavé to remind you where your beads will be.

Step 4

Take an appropriate, sharp scorper. From the line you've marked, cut the metal away from the sides at a 45-degree angle. Leave metal in between for the beads. I like to start around the edges to create a frame or box. Then I can work from the outside in.

Step 5

Use a burr or a scorper to cut out the metal between each stone seat. All that's left should be your beads. This time, you have the added fun of figuring out which of the beads in between will hold each stone in. If you take too much metal away, there won't be anything to hold them in.

Step 6

Burr any flash away to clean out the seats. Sit the stones down, table flush with the surface of the metal.

Step 7

Use your sharp scorper to nudge the beads over. Keep alternating to ensure your stone stays straight. Make sure the beads are firmly down and the stone is rock solid. Move to the next stone and repeat.

Step 8

You will have to sit in and set a few stones at the same time. Be aware that stones are staying straight and aren't tipping up.

Step 9

Take an appropriately sized beader and gently rock in a circular motion to create a bead over the stone. You may have to do this strategically to lock stones into place before beading over others.

Step 10

Use scorpers to clean behind the beads, making the corners nice and crisp. Go along the straight edge with a sharp scorper to create a sharp, bright cut.

Summary

Pavé is a very rewarding method of setting. It sticks to a rigid formula, making the technique simple to understand, but very tricky to master. One false move can ruin a few hours' work; careless cutting away or flippant beading can bring it all down and cause a great deal of distress. But don't be dismayed while you learn. You can't advance without making mistakes. It's the heartache of a simple error that stays with you and spurs you on to better things. Once you master this method, you'll become addicted to it like so many other setters all around the world.

Vanilla Ink – Pair of pavé rings. A feat of engineering, this remodelled pair of wedding rings were created using ninety-two diamonds, ranging from 2.5mm to 1.5mm. They were painstakingly laid out so that each ring looked consistent with not too much fluctuation in stone size. (Vanilla Ink)

CHANNEL AND MICROCLAW SETTING

Channel Setting

This is where things step up a bit and become more advanced. Channel setting is the technique that took me the longest to master, simply because of the accuracy and dexterity required. One slip with a scorper and it's ruined, one misplaced push and it's smashed, one wayward movement with the burr and you've cut through the wall.

I can understand why some jewellers want to stay away from this style; it genuinely is difficult, particularly with shaped stones. Think of channel setting baguettes lengthways, you're putting something straight into a piece that has curvature. The level of accuracy required to burr a seat for that stone is pretty intense and not for the faint-hearted!

Theory

Channel setting is where we take two walls of metal (either pre-made or cut into the piece), and set stones between them. It is probably most like bezel, in that the wall is folded over each stone, but far more complex. A burr (or scorper if you're particularly old school) must be used to create a ledge on which the stone is seated. To set the stone, we must tuck it under the wall, before it is pushed over and finished. While all this sounds relatively simple in theory, the actual method is incredibly tricky.

LEFT: **White gold microclaw earrings. Trademark work by McCaul Goldsmiths, the sweeping elegance of these earrings is complemented by the deadly accurate setting work. (Keith Leighton)**

Ryan Nelson – Single stone channel set ring. An unusual little ring, but don't let that take away from the craftsmanship. Channel setting is usually done with multiple stones; however, this beautiful 'Teardrop' ring carries only a solitary diamond. The result is subtle yet eye-catching. (Ryan Nelson)

Before you start

Every stone you will set has to be placed at exactly the same level, angle and position or the client's eye will be drawn towards it. A stone that sits even slightly off will leap out towards you and scream to be reset, which often is a luxury you do not have when it comes to channel setting. Although completely secure when finished and rock-solid, the stones are essentially held in by the bare minimum amount of metal. Saying that, the metal that holds the stones in must be significant enough and not paper-thin. This is one of the most common mistakes. In the goldsmith's eagerness to push over and secure the stones, too much metal is filed away or overworked, resulting either in it flaking away when finished or the ring coming back into your workshop well before its sell-by date! Channel setting requires a great deal of patience and dexterity. Be prepared to make catastrophic errors! But understand that this is all part of the learning curve. You can't learn until you mess up a few times, but when you get it right, the end result and satisfaction will stay with you for a long time.

Method

Step 1
The initial, set-up part of this is similar to pavé, so will feel familiar. Use dividers to mark a straight line in the metal. Then set them to a fraction over the size of stone you are using. Mark along the line. The idea is to have the stones as close together as possible without actually touching. Mark where you want your stones to sit with a centre punch (or similar). Drill down and burr out the holes to an appropriate size (see Chapter 3 for instructions, although this is slightly different). For a 3mm stone, this should be about 2mm–2.5mm, for example. If you open it up to the same dimensions as the stones, we will have no ledge to tuck the stones under! This is where opening up holes slightly differs from other techniques, as we don't want to sit the stones down into the metal just yet.

Step 2
Using dividers again, lightly score or mark a line *exactly* on the lip of the holes. This is your guideline for where to cut the metal away to. Now we need to clean away all unnecessary metal. Use a combination of burrs, scorpers and files to remove the metal up to your outer guidelines.

Step 3
The channel should now be cut, looking crisp and clean. The stones should sit comfortably *on top* of the channel. If they sit into it, you have cleaned away too much. Use a bearing cutter to create space for a notch inside the channel for the stone to tuck into. For a 3mm stone, use a 2mm, for example. Using the same size of burr as the stone will be too big, and will result in you damaging the nice straight outside wall of the setting. Burr gently and accurately into one side of the channel. Flip around and do the exact same to the other side. Make sure you have created the same size of notch on either side and that they match each other. If they're slightly off, the stone will not sit in place.

Step 4
I always start with the middle stone and work my way to the outsides. That way, if I have miscalculated and cut away too much metal and made the channel too long, I can put a little space in between each stone, which is a little less catastrophic than having a gaping space at one end. Slide and attempt to tuck the stone into place. Do this by slotting it into one of the burred-out notches at an angle, then try to get it to sit straight and locate into the opposite side. If it doesn't go, *do not* force it into the seat. You could end up chipping the stone. Burr away a little bit more under the lip of the channel to allow the stone to locate in nicely. This may be on just one side or both. At this point, you can choose to locate all stones in place before pushing the walls over or go along

one by one. I prefer the latter as I feel more in control.

Step 5

Once the stone is in place, looking straight and even, you can begin to push the edge of the metal over. This process locks the stone in its seat. I like to make sure the stone is solid, then move on to setting the next one. Once I've put them all in place, I go back and make sure the walls are firmly over, looking even, but not squashed to within a millimetre of their lives. Once you get to the end stones, things get a little trickier, as you may (depending on the look of the ends) have to tuck them under from three sides instead of two. This can prove quite frustrating, so go slowly and be careful not to burr away too much metal. When it comes to this, I leave the second from last stone out, which allows me to get the burr in without damaging the previous stone or walls of the metal. Now, once I've created space, I

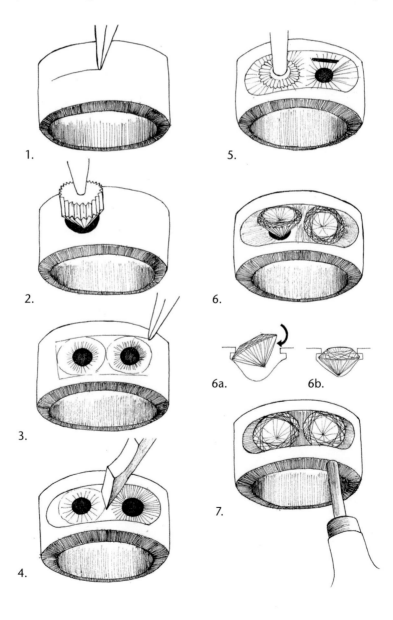

Channel setting step by step. (Jennifer Colquhoun)

HINTS AND TIPS

- Remember to mark out and scribe on a rough template of where the walls should be and so on, as this will prevent you from taking away too much metal.
- You can use your pliers to set and secure stones in place (I know, right?)… just be gentle!
- When marking out for the row of stones, bear in mind that once the stones are burred down and seated, they will be closer than they were on the surface. That's the physics of a curve for you.

can slot the stone in the second from last hole, then slide it into its own space under the end ledge. Then you can pop the second from last stone in, which is now technically the last stone.

Step 6

Finish with a gentle file to the outside and inside edge, keeping the metal crisp and even, without taking too much away. Think of it like finishing a bezel setting on the outside, and lining pavé setting with the inner edge.

Summary

Channel setting is a style that has lasted the ages. It is clean, crisp and consistently popular.

Vanilla Ink – Channel set platinum ring. A remodelling commission where we were asked to remove the stones from an old 18ct white gold ring to reset them in platinum. A happy client! (Vanilla Ink)

When done properly and to a high level, the results can be stunning. However, there is absolutely no place to hide when it comes to this style of setting. A poorly set stone will leap out from the piece and haunt you in your dreams. I myself have struggled with keeping the level or angle of the stones consistent, and when I was learning, I constantly made the wall too thin. This meant when it came to finishing, it wobbled all over the place, like some kind of jewellery jelly on a plate. As mentioned in the tips, you can set traditionally with push tools, or you can be bold and use pliers to secure the stones tightly (my old boss would probably throw things at me for doing this). The methods are different but the technique required remains the same. Sit the stone down, same level and angle as the last, and secure the stone without taking too much metal away. Channel setting requires a great deal of patience and dexterity. Be prepared to make catastrophic errors! But understand that this is all part of the learning curve. You can't learn until you mess up a few times, but when you get it right, the end result and satisfaction feels good.

Microclaw Setting

This is the new kid on the block, one that became popular a few years ago but has grown in popularity and is now widely seen within jewellery. A variation of claw and pavé setting, microclaw is basically the same technique as the latter but *without* outer walls. It is one of the most intricate and tricky techniques you can learn as a stone setter. As the name suggests, everything is done on a very small scale, with small, round stones on an incredibly small, technical basis.

Theory

Microclaw is all about what you take away and what you leave behind. Which usually isn't a lot, as the name suggests. This again lives within our 'advanced' section and for good reason.

Murazzo – Double row microclaw marquise ring. Outstanding manufacturing again by Michael Muratore, this exceptional marquise ring is complemented by a double row of microclaw set diamonds. Simply amazing. (Michael Muratore)

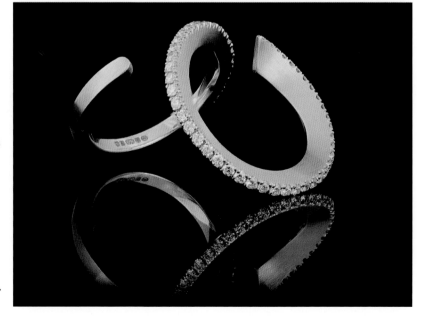

McCaul Goldsmiths – Rose gold diamond cocktail ring. You really don't need me to say much here at all. I'll just say wow and leave you to marvel at this incredible ring. (Keith Leighton)

The style is usually performed with small stones (hence the name) and requires deadly accuracy. You are leaving such tiny slivers of metal behind, that even the tiniest of fractions out with measuring or cutting can devastate a job. It's a style of setting that requires not only experience but a great deal of skill and patience, too.

Before you start

Get prepared to go cross-eyed! I would strongly recommend using optivisors for this method, as it requires absolute precision. While setting tiny stones means that not a lot of metal is required to secure them, it also allows far more room for error. Similar to pavé, microclaw also throws up the choice to share the claws or split them. As there are two different styles to microclaw, each tutorial will be allocated a different method to explore.

Different Techniques

Castle Setting

Up close and personal with some castle setting, Ryan Nelson shows us exactly how it should be done. (Ryan Nelson)

Method

Step 1

Use dividers to mark a straight line in the metal. For shared claws, it's like pavé in that we want the stones to be tight together. This gives the claw the best chance of securing both stones in place.

Mark where you want your stones to sit with a centre punch (or similar). Drill down and burr out the holes to an appropriate size (*see* Chapter 3 for instructions).

Step 2

Take a setting burr (2mm for a 2mm stone and so on) and gently cut a seat for each stone. You want the table of the stone to sit approximately just above the surface of the metal. Clean out the previous seat as you go along. Once all your seats have been drilled, take your scribe and gently mark where the metal is to be removed. This will be across the stone and straight down the middle. Now use needle files and a variety of burrs to clean away the metal. Remember, what you leave behind is used to set the stone. As you look at the side of the ring, you should have a series of 'U' shapes filed and burred out. Remember, you can add a decorative scallop to make the setting look elegant. Check that the sizes of your claws are even and are pretty much square in shape.

Step 3

At this stage, you would highly polish your decorative scallop as you won't be able to get into it once the stones are set. Once done, make sure your stones are seated and sitting level.

Step 4

Time to set. Start at the end claws. Make sure you have taken a saw cut down so that they are in proportion to the rest of the claws. Use a flat scorper (ground so that it is shallow and sharp) to lean them over towards the stone. Now time to make a choice... do you use a push tool, or do you take your snipe nose pliers and gently squeeze the claws over from the side?

Step 5

Go along the rest of the settings, using pliers or a push tool to push them tight in between the stones. Again, it helps to think of this like pavé – we want to get that claw as far in between each stone so that it touches both and keeps them secure. The stones should now be locked in place. Be sure to check that they're sitting straight and even.

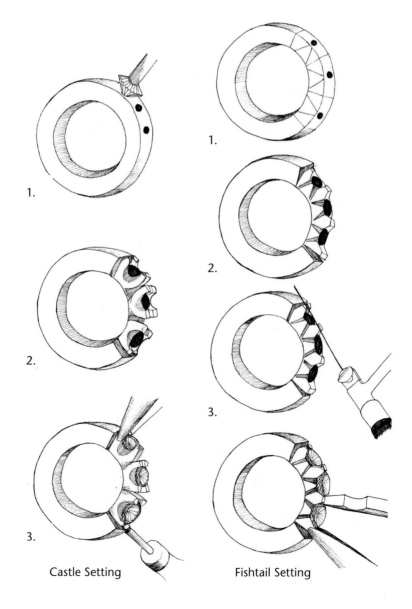

Microclaw setting step by step. (Jennifer Colquhoun)

Castle Setting

Fishtail Setting

Step 6
Finish by filing up any bruising from the pliers and setting. Gently use a needle file to clean up claws, taking away any sharp edges and making sure they look even. It won't need much as the polish on the buff will soften them and finish them naturally.

Fishtail Setting

Ryan Nelson – Fishtail setting up close. Again, some close-up magic by Ryan Nelson. Note the care and attention taken over the fine details. (Ryan Nelson)

Method

Step 1
Use dividers to mark a straight line in the metal. Unlike the previous method, we want the stones to have a slight gap between them. This allows us to split the claw. Mark where you want your stones to sit with a centre punch (or similar). Drill down and burr out the holes to an appropriate size (*see* Chapter 3 for instructions). Take a setting burr (2mm for a 2mm stone and so on) and gently cut a seat for each stone. You want the table of the stone to sit approximately just above the surface of the metal. Clean out the previous seat as you go along.

Step 2
Now we get decorative. We want the claw to look like a fishtail, but directly underneath the stone will be cut metal that comes to a point. It is very tricky but simplified if you stick to a routine.

We need to use our saw blade to mark a series of lines along the side of the ring. If you're not comfortable using your saw to do this, mark it with a scribe or similar. The simplest way to describe it is to make each claw a fishtail shape with a 'mountain' in between. Where the stone sits, mark an inverted 'V'. The bottom of each 'V' should meet with the next stone's one on the bottom of the shank. I am incredibly glad we have illustrations to go with this!

Step 3
Now that we have given ourselves guidelines to follow, it's time to go cutting. Use a lozenge graver or spitzstick to cut a crisp, precise line where you've marked. Once you start to do this, you'll see the claws appearing and get a better picture of how it will eventually look. Check that the sizes of your claws are even, remembering that they will be split into two.

They should be rectangular in shape. Keep going until you've cut and prepared all stones. At this point, a crisp, square needle file can help to straighten everything up.

Step 4
Just like with the castle setting, now is the time to high polish the ring. As much as the graver will create a bright cut, there's no substitute for a clean final buff.

Step 5
Now for the tricky part. We need to split the claw. Use an 8/0 saw blade to do this, to give the claws a good chance of remaining sturdy. An uneven cut here can ruin the job, be careful. Mark with gentle saw cuts to ensure you're cutting correctly before sawing down completely. If you want, scribe a line down the side to keep you accurate.

Step 6
Time to set. Start at the end claws. Make sure you have taken a saw cut down so that they are in proportion to the rest of the claws. Use a flat

Lado's Jewellery Studio – Castle setting. I am in constant awe of the level of perfection and detail that Lado constantly executes. It's possible he isn't actually human. This is just stunning. (Lado Shvili)

HINTS AND TIPS

- As with most techniques that require the removal of metal, try marking out just after you've drilled the holes to see how much you need to remove. Draw on where your claws will be and perhaps draw with a marker where the metal is to be removed. This may help you at the start until you get used to the technique.
- Don't forget to high polish the job before setting. Once the stones are in, there's no way of getting in to finish the metal other than removing the stones… *disaster!*
- If you're feeling brave, you can give the setting a squeeze on the top using half round pliers. Be careful not to push too hard and chip the stones!
- When cutting out your decoration, you can always use a square or triangular needle file to keep the cutting even.
- Treat shared microclaw just like you would a normal claw set ring. Setting requires a gentle touch, with a lot of going back and forth to make sure stones sit straight and are locked in completely.

scorper to lean them over towards the stone. Now take your snipe nose pliers and gently squeeze the claws over from the side. You can use a narrow push tool here if you're nervous about using pliers!

Step 7

Go along the rest of the stones, first pushing them as we would normally set a claw, then use your flat scorper to gently lean the claws one way towards one stone, then the other way towards its neighbour. Think of this method

as the exact same way as splitting the bead for pavé. We have to nudge them forward and to the side to be sure of setting properly. The stones should now be locked in place. Be sure to check that they're sitting straight and even.

Step 8

Finish by filing up any bruising from the pliers and setting. Gently use a needle file to clean up the claws, taking away any sharp edges and making sure they look even. It won't need

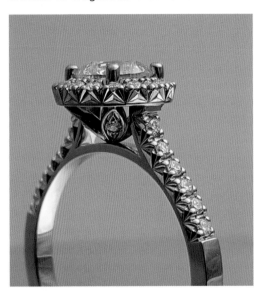

Lado's Jewellery Studio – Castle setting. Again, this is so incredible it looks like a CAD render. Nobody should be allowed to be this skilled; it isn't fair on the rest of us. These images are simply breathtaking. (Lado Shvili)

much as the polish on the buff will soften them and finish them naturally.

Summary

I really, really love this style of setting. It's completely self-taught, but I reckon that goes for the majority of us setters. We saw a style, loved it, then figured out how to do it, refining as we went along. I do enjoy both methods, and I love how cutting away in different styles alters the look entirely, but if I had to choose, I'd go for fishtail. You can go to town and way over the top with your decoration, cut away here there and everywhere to create sharp, glistening facets that catch the light and sparkle alongside the stones. Experiment yourself and see what you come up with.

SHAPED STONES

Usually what follows setting round stones, is to venture into the world of shaped stones. And what this means is introducing yourself to the dreaded corners! A shaped stone is a different animal entirely. Firstly, we don't have shaped burrs yet, meaning we have to hand-cut using scorpers.

To me, I have no problem with this, as I was taught to cut round settings by hand. While I cursed the jewellers who taught me under my breath, I now fully acknowledge it's held me in good stead for cutting shapes. Using scorpers is a learned craft, but one that opens up the possibilities of flush setting an odd-shaped stone.

LEFT: **McCaul Goldsmiths – Green stone ring. What a beauty! McCaul's emerald cut bezel setting is just perfect. Look at the lovely strong bezel and the crisp, straight lines. (Keith Leighton)**

Even flush setting an old cut diamond can require a bit of thought, so it's good to have this particular skill in your armoury. Couple that with becoming a wizard with a 0.5mm ball burr in your pendant drill, and you're there! Sort of.

Theory

To set a shaped stone, we need to respect and deal with corners. A crisp, pointy peak is a true thing of beauty but is perilous to us setters. It is the natural weak point of the stone, the most obvious place it will snap, shear or crumble. If only everything was as easy to set as a round stone. Using a lovely, sharp setting burr to cut a nice, round seat for your nice round stone. Drop it in, get the metal over, go ahead and finish.

Now suffer the horror of shaped stones…

Vanilla Ink – Commissions. We get all sorts of jobs at Vanilla Ink, from the simple round stone to the more complex and unusual shapes. (Vanilla Ink)

There is no lovely sharp burr where we're going. This is all done with your fair hands, using a wide variety of tools and techniques. This is proper old school, harking back to the days before you lucky lot grew up with electric drills and pre-made burrs (to be fair, I grew up in this era too, but as I said, I was forced to learn hand-cutting).

This is proper, handmade jewellery, skilfully cut out to the most accurate of margins and set with immaculate precision. There's no hiding place here and an error can cost you an entire job. But apart from all of that, it's fun! Honestly, don't be put off!

We're going to explore a variety of stone shapes, to be set in a variety of styles. We will try to cover as broad a spectrum as possible, using common shapes of stones with popular styles of setting. Each of these shapes and styles will be entirely interchangeable, for example the principles of rubover apply to all stone shapes with corners and so on. Some are trickier than others, and some demand more accuracy.

Before you start

The answer to the question 'Why is my stone not going in?' is *always* 'It's the damn corners, you fool!' The first lesson of Corner Club is 'clean out those corners', then go back and

How incredible is this green tourmaline ring? I mean, talk about the star of the show! The stone is expertly set using robust claws that are finished and shaped perfectly to compliment the stone's shape. (Vanilla Ink)

We often get to use a variety of shaped stones when creating client commissions here at Vanilla Ink. Beautiful bespoke jewellery that makes an impact like this will live forever. (Vanilla Ink)

make sure they're a little more cleaned out. Even slight margins, and we're talking tenths, one-hundredths of a millimetre, can make a difference. If you recall our chat about pressure points in the Claw Setting section, the danger here is multiplied by a huge amount. Corners can crack if you so much as look at them in a funny way (obviously this is a *joke*, duh), so we must learn to treat them with the respect they deserve.

Also, while I've prattled on and on about patience and precision throughout this manual, we now need to ramp it up even more. My advice is to take your time while you're learning, as this methodical approach will help you out as you progress. Setting shapes can frustrate the most patient of jewellers, please get into the mindset that this will take time to master and you'll be fine.

Different Techniques

Bezel setting corners

If I can recommend one thing to you, it would be to create a bezel that slots over the stone, then add a seat for it. The pros to this style, although tricky to match the seat to the setting, far outweigh the cons when it comes to cutting a seat by hand. I find that scoring and folding creates a much better fit for corners, rather than using scorpers. You may disagree, but I won't hold it against you.

Method

Step 1

Whatever shape your stone is, build the bezel to the outer dimensions of the stone, which should slot through perfectly without catching any of the sides. Then create a mini bezel, mirroring the inside shape of the setting exactly, so that it requires a little push to slot inside at the correct height. When making it, make sure you create a little chamfer so that it's a proper seat for the stone. Solder it in, and you're ready to go.

Step 2

As we've already discovered, square burrs for jewellery don't exist yet. This is why we patiently created a perfectly shaped bezel, with the seat all ready and waiting to accept the stone. Sit the stone in place and check all is okay. Sometimes you can get excess solder where the seat is; carefully remove it with a 0.5mm ball burr to allow the stone to sit if it's affected. On the flip side of that, please make sure that enough solder has run into each of your corners. When you go to set, any fresh air will be exposed, ruining the setting.

Step 3

I know of some setters who like to start with the corners and work their way back from there. I'm the opposite; I prefer to begin in between the corners (the four flat sides of a square stone, for example) as I feel this allows the stone to be locked into place. The corners are then easier to deal with if the gem isn't being a shiny rock 'n' roll star, flipping around everywhere as we try to push. Push the wall over as you would for a round, working your way towards the corners.

Step 4

Time to work the corners. When we set corners, we have to make sure we push against the metal perpendicular to where the push tool is. If you push over a little so that there is no resistance from the other corner, the edge will fold in on itself, causing all sorts of drama and chaos. The idea is to compress the sides of the corner against each other, rather than tucking under themselves. Push as much as you can until no metal moves anymore. Gently, and I mean gently, remove a little of the weight from the outside wall. A safety-back needle file is ideal for this. A couple of flicks with the file should be sufficient to allow you to push a little more of the corners against each other. Keep this up until the corners compress against each other, creating a beautiful crisp corner on both the inside and outside. Just please, please, be careful not to file away too much metal. Do it little by little until you get the gist of what's required.

Lado's Jewellery Studio – Bezel set blue stone with pear shape. Yet more stunning work by Lado, with the added double whammy of huge pear shapes as accent stones. Beautiful bezel setting. (Lado Shvili)

Step 5

Finishing corners requires a deft touch. Take a very sharp flat scorper and cut a smooth, bright cut, making sure you don't remove too much metal and cause devastation. If you've pushed the corners correctly, the scorper should just accentuate the lovely 90-degree angle that's been created, while making it nice and shiny at the same time. Finish with a smooth burnisher as you would a round stone.

'V' claws

Setting a 'V' claw is very similar to pushing over the corners of a bezel. However, the lack of metal in between the claws allows us to explore a few more options of how to secure the stone, as well as different ways of finishing them. Precision is required in their manufacture; however, soldering them onto a setting is easier than rounds, as they 'cuddle' each corner, keeping them straight and true.

Method

Step 1

Making 'V' claws is a relatively simple process of scoring and folding, then soldering them shut. Cut and fold a strip of metal (length determined by the height of your setting), until it perfectly mirrors the corner of your stone. Squares, pear shape or trilliants, for example, can all have differently angled corners. The width of the metal you begin with determines if you have a narrow, delicate 'V', or a wide, definite one. Assemble your setting and you're ready to go.

Step 2

As we have no sides to deal with, only corners, this simplifies things. However, we have a few options, here. We can push them over just as we would for a round. This presents a couple of options to finish them off. When we cut them back, we can either leave them flat across or take our scorper to cut a nice corner. Either is acceptable. The former is a far easier way to finish and my preferred method. Although it is flat across the stone, it still appears as if it has a corner. Our other choice is to trim the claw way down so that just a sliver peeks over the stone's girdle. We would then treat this in the

A signature sweeping spectrum cluster ring by Scott that slides away from deep blue sapphire to crisp pale aquamarine. Note the lovely angular 'V' claw that enhances the rich London Blue Topaz pear shape centre stone. (Vanilla Ink)

same way as a bezel corner, gently nudging either side over the stone, carefully filing away until the corner is set. Again, use a sharp scorper to enhance the corner and give it a bright cut.

Non 'V' claws

Essentially, a great deal of the previous section can be transported over here, as well as cross-referencing the claw setting chapter. We're looking at creating claws in the normal style, except we have to leave room for the corners to poke into. There's a couple of ways to do this, both of them straightforward enough and easy to execute. There's a little debate from purists, who claim that a round claw has no place on a stone with straight edges; however, these people are from the Dark Ages.

Method

Step 1

There are two ways here, feel free to choose whichever way you like. My preferred method

Ryan Nelson – Princess cut set with talon claws. Setting corners can be scary, but Ryan shows no fear here! A masterclass in how to mix the strong with the subtle, the talon-style claws work beautifully with the amazing princess cut diamond. (Ryan Nelson)

is to saw straight down the claw, then go in with a sharp square needle file, which creates a 'V' shaped slot all the way down the claw. This allows it to be located onto the corner of the setting when manufacturing, and also space for the corner of the stone to slot into. The other technique requires you to create a groove into the claw after the setting has been built with either a setting burr turned 90 degrees or a 0.5mm ball burr. It can also be tidied up with a scorper.

Step 2

As for setting and finishing, we simply treat it as we would a round, only this time we maybe take a little more care when pushing the claws over. Just be wary that the pressure of the claws is directly over the weakest point of the stone, which must be treated with care and respect.

Emerald and Asscher cuts

A little shout out here for the emerald or Asscher cut claw setting, which requires no faffing around with corners, grooves or folding. Simply mimic the flat edge of the diagonal 'corners' of the stone, using a nice rectangular strip for the claw. Setting is simple; treat it like a round stone. There's no risk either of a fragile corner, making it a less dangerous shape to set. Finish with an elegant taper, which mirrors the almost triangular facet that these kinds of stones have at each claw.

Flush setting shapes

And so we come to the incredibly tricky section. I honestly think that flush setting a shaped stone is one of the most difficult things you'll do as a setter. You have to cut a deadly accurate hole out of solid metal, using hand tools for the majority of the process. A slip of the scorper ruins the job. So does an errant nudge in the wrong place with your push tool. Hopefully, by now you understand the precision required for flush setting; the step up to shaped stones is a pretty hefty one indeed.

Method

Step 1

Open up the metal in the usual manner, except we're going to apply a bit of thought. Let's say we were setting a 3mm square stone; after drilling through, I would use a 2.5mm setting burr to create a seat as if you were setting a round. Don't be tempted to use a 3mm round burr as you're setting a 3mm square stone, the cutting action with your scorper will damage the sides of the hole and open it up too much. Trust me, I've tried it.

Step 2

Start to cut the seat for the stone. If you want, use a scribe to mark a rough square on the top of the metal as a guide. This isn't just a tip for the novice; I will still do this, no matter what shape of stone I'm setting. Now comes the tricky part, as we use scorpers to cut a hole that is the exact same size as the stone. Usually, this will naturally be done with a slight taper down the hole, so the stone will not fall all the way through. Start with a lozenge graver to dictate where the corners are, then go back and forth between that and a flat scorper, cutting tiny slivers of metal away at a time, until you have a crisp hole with straight edges, but not any bigger than the stone.

Step 3

Once you've opened up the hole to the correct dimensions, use a 0.5mm ball burr to make a seat for the stone to sit on. It's also used to clean out the corners. This is probably the most important thing you'll do. We almost want to employ the channel setting technique here, creating a ledge all the way around onto which the stone will slot. The burr should create a little space under each edge, as well as creating a little cave or pocket where the corners will be. Experience tells me to completely remove metal from here, as I've chipped many a flush set stone with corners after not cleaning enough metal away. The point has been sat in tight against metal, then once you try to set, *crack*, and that's the end of

Lado's Jewellery Studio – Shaped flush setting. Faultless setting once more. It's just perfect, it really is. Don't talk, just look. (Lado Shvili)

the stone. Burring away a little extra does not affect how the stone sits and relieves the pressure on the most vulnerable part(s) of the stone.

Step 4

The stone's table should sit just about level with the metal. It should also be located with no gaps showing, especially around the corners. Make sure it's rock-solid as a loose stone is a pest to set. Begin setting, using the same flush setting technique as the round stone, and the identical process as shaped bezel. Start in the middle of one of the sides, move opposite, then push on the remaining two. This hopefully locks the stone in place. Keep pushing the straight edges over, gently working towards the corners. Use the overlapping technique to keep the edge smooth and even. Now for the corners. This is the most delicate part. Gently nudge the corners over, taking care not to touch the fragile stone. When the edges meet up, use the edge of the push tool to create a crease or fold

for the corner. Finish off in a similar style to the rounds, taking care at the corners each time. If you have to use a scorper to create a crisp line at the corner, then do so.

Backholing

This is the term we use for creating decorative shapes underneath or behind the setting. Think of the inside of a ring shank. When setting rounds, we just leave the nice round we've drilled, thank you very much. However, if we are setting square stones, then take the time to create square holes behind the setting. A piece of jewellery should not just look amazing from the top, every single angle of the damn thing should be perfect, professional and precise. Even if we're flush setting a pear shape, the hole underneath should be shaped to mirror the stone. You need to become quite proficient with your saw and a thin blade. You almost use the blade as a file, carefully shaving away metal to open up and make a perfect hole.

You may think this seems unnecessary, but top class jewellery requires attention to detail and the highest of finishes. Being great at backholing will mean more work for you, my friend.

Tension setting shapes

Our next method follows on nicely from flush setting. It's very similar, in that we need to create exact, beautifully cut away metal for stones to locate into. Again, I'll draw your attention toward the need to clean out where the corners will sit, especially for tension setting. Think of the force that is holding the stones in place, and imagine the pressure those delicate little corners will already be under, never mind if they have a poorly cut space to house them with lumps of metal perilously pressing on them.

So how do you do it?

To be honest, there's really not a lot to say here. The method is the exact same as setting rounds, except we need to be a little more cute with removing metal. Once we've used the setting burr, you need to use a 0.5mm ball burr to make the straight side fit. Sometimes, the point of a shaped stone is placed in the metal for tension setting. It takes a brave and experienced setter to get away with this. Be sure to burr a fair amount away so that the point is completely in and not balancing precariously in between the metal. As for setting, apply the same technique as for round stones.

Channel setting straight edges

As if channel setting rounds wasn't hard enough, we now have to factor in straight edges! While for round stones we can burr a seat for each individual stone, straight edges mean we have to create a ledge all the way along our channel. This allows the corners to slide in and sit right beside the adjacent stone. While this is a

step up from rounds, if you have good pendant drill and burr control, it should go okay for you. But, if we add setting baguettes lengthways into the mix, this is a different story altogether. If it's a flat pendant, then fine, but if we're setting into a ring, this poses a bit of an issue. The ring is naturally curved; the long baguette is straight. The level of precision here is insane. Burr it too deep, it looks terrible; too shallow, the ends are going to burst through the top of the walls. It's satisfying when you nail it, though!

Method

Step 1
The set-up for this is just the same as for rounds. Cut the channel, make it crisp and even, then you're ready to cut the ledge. Take the exact setting burr you would use for rounds, only this time we are not burring 5, 7, 9 or whatever individual seats, we're taking the ledge all the way along the length of the channel on both sides. I like to scribe a line with my dividers as I feel any help here at all is beneficial. I can carefully work my way along the line burring slowly and evenly to create a long shelf.

Step 2
Technically, if you've done this correctly, you can slot all stones in at this point, sliding them in and along to their new homes. I suppose this is the one upside to this method. To answer your question (because I know you'll ask it), there's no reason why you can't do this for rounds. I just feel that burring the individual holes prevents the stones from rocking side to side. Once the stones are in, again, set in the same manner as rounds. If you have trouble sliding them all in, set one at a time like rounds also.

Setting baguettes

Baguettes are rarely the star of the show, more often the pretty sideshow, off to one side and

You can't beat a bit of bling bling! This remodelled ring used the client's heirloom materials, including round and oval diamonds, and those tricky little square cuts channel set down the shank. Diamond heaven!

Shivani Goldsmiths – Shaped channel setting. Aren't these rings beautiful? The execution of the setting is flawless, and believe me, this is not an easy task! Look at how straight, sharp and crisp they are. Outstanding work. (Richard Valencia)

Ryan Nelson – 'V' claws and baguettes. Two fine examples here by Ryan. Firstly, the incredible deep, rich sapphire held in by perfect 'V' claws, then onto the baguette accent stones. Solid, rigid and straight as a row of soldiers! (Ryan Nelson)

Baguettes, either straight or tapered, can often appear quite easy to set but can throw up lots of problems. You must get all four corners perfect and have each stone sitting at the correct angle, not tilted or twisted. (Vanilla Ink)

enhancing what's in the centre. But that doesn't mean we don't show them the same love and care. A well-made baguette setting still takes time and requires accuracy. They're more than often small and delicate too, so creating mini settings to strict measurements poses its own problems.

So how do you do it?

Baguettes are usually set by two flaps at the end of the stone, a bit like a semi rubover. It isn't fully encased, just the ends, leaving the two longer sides exposed. It doesn't matter if it's tapered or straight, the same rules apply. Think of it as pushing over the straight edge of a square setting, each flap gets nudges over until flat against the stone, before being cut back,

then finished. They're usually filed up neat and flat, but this isn't always the case. A sturdier flap can be used, which is either pre-shaped or filed up afterwards.

Summary
Setting shaped stones really is a step up from mere rounds. But don't let that hold you back. After all, shaped stones do exist and make up a huge amount of jewellery out there. If you've got the skills to set rounds, there is absolutely no reason why you can't step up and deal with straight edges and corners. As with all methods, practise hard first, then practise some more. You may find that it's not so daunting after all! Just think how awesome your designs will be now that you can factor shapes into them!

TAKING IT TO THE NEXT LEVEL

An honourable mention here goes to the jobs that require guile, craft and initiative. The kind of design that's unteachable or you don't find in a manual. There are times where we must use a mix of setting methods, a stone may be crying out for a 'V' claw at its nose, but a bezel on its bum. There are jobs where a strong, dominant border of metal truly enhances the stone. This may need a combination of bezel and flush setting. And then there is the jewellery that simply just looks better with a couple of techniques thrown at it, not for practical reasons, but mainly for aesthetics. Go ahead, have fun and mix it up a little. There is no rule book to say that you can't use combined methods or a few styles in one piece, and don't let anyone tell you otherwise.

LEFT: **Polly Wales – 'Enchanted City' skull pendant. I am in complete awe of what Polly does… her jewellery is mind-blowing. Other people around the world have grasped the concept of casting with stones in place, but nobody does it like her. She's amazing. (James Firman)**

Setting stones from the back

Did you know you can pop a stone in from the back? Who knew? Well, me obviously. Yes, doing things in reverse can offer up a perfectly clean look from the front, while all the hard work has gone on underneath for a change. For example, to give the look of flush setting, set up as normal, drilling all the way through (say 2.5mm for a 3mm stone), then flip the job around and burr down with a setting burr from the *back* of the job instead of the top. Be careful not to go all the way through. Slot the stone in and use back cuts (like raising the grain with a scorper) to secure the stone, or (if the stone can take heat) solder a bearer wire to hold the stone in place. It's not very common to set this way, but there's certainly a time and a place for it, and it is worth exploring.

Using Wax To Set Stones

Theory

Setting stones in wax completely reverses the stone setting process. Usually, pieces of jewellery are made, then once everything has been assembled, stone setting is pretty much the last thing to do. This method adds stones way at the beginning of the process, flipping it around on its head and completely defying tradition. Adding stones at the start creates unpredictability, allowing beautifully organic jewellery to be manufactured. It's the imperfections that

Ryan Nelson – Green stone bezel set. I've set like this on many occasions. It requires a blend of both bezel and flush setting to achieve the bold look to it. Ryan makes it look easy here. (Ryan Nelson)

Angela O'Keefe – Blue stone 18ct yellow gold ring. A lovely little mix of both channel and claw setting here. Angela's beautiful design in 18ct yellow gold looks amazing with the unique setting style. (Sharon Duffin)

McCaul Goldsmiths – Purple stone bezel and claw set. More of a common mix, McCaul Goldsmith's trilliant cut setting used bezel setting at the wide end, with a 'V' claw on the nose. (Keith Leighton)

Polly Wales – 'Empress' ring. A treat for your eyes! Look at the lovely spectrum of colours, but also pay attention to the accuracy and patience that go into placing each of these stones on the ring, making sure they are held in place perfectly. (James Firman)

Polly Wales – Cast not set ring. It's the imperfections that do it for me. The eroded, erratic look of the whole ring is simply beautiful, accentuated by the variety of colours used. Lovely. (James Firman)

make this style so alluring, allowing the most striking of pieces to be created.

So how do you do it?

Okay, I am not an expert here at all. I've only done this a handful of times, and even then, it's not been perfect. I am a novice when it comes to this process, we don't have in-house casting facilities at Vanilla Ink, so that particular part of the wizardry is done by sourcing outside experts. We use the fantastically talented Circinn Studios in Dundee; Charlie McManus dedicates patience and time to learning new methods for gem-in-place casting, ever experimenting and striving for perfection.

Saying that, we can look at the principles of the process and try to add a little insight into how it's done. Pioneers like Polly Wales really have taken this process and made it their own. By simply looking at even just one of Polly's pieces, you can see the creativity, vision and skill that has made her one of the leading exponents of this kind of jewellery. While we can boil the method down to simple instructions, the actual execution is far from straightfor-

ward. Experts have taken years to finely hone their craft; don't think you'll become a genius overnight!

Right, I'll admit it. I never understood how this worked. I genuinely thought it was witchcraft. I couldn't picture what happens to the stones once the wax had burnt out. My head told me they should all fall down, as there was no wax to hold them in place anymore. In my mind, they were suspended in fresh air, being held up by some magic force. I wondered if you could only set with wax if you owned a black cat and wore a pointy hat.

Once explained, it makes clear and perfect sense. The stone must be exposed to investment both top *and* bottom. This means the hole where your stone is to be set has to be drilled all the way through, and by a considerable amount. Failure to open it up enough may result in the investment snapping when hardened, resulting in a botched cast. Picture the investment being poured in, pinching the stone from both top and bottom. To help, hold something in between your thumb and forefinger. This is what it'll look like after burnout. In my mind, I see a stalactite and stalagmite joining, holding a sparkly gem in between. Without

**Polly Wales – Skull ring. I adore skulls, so this is a perfect mix for me, personally. I love the ideas
Polly comes up with, but I reckon this might be a favourite of mine for a long time. (James Firman)**

ABOVE AND OPPOSITE: **Maud Traon – Electroformed jewellery. Maud's work looks like it fell here from another planet. It is striking, unusual and just incredible. She creates real statement pieces that I am in absolute awe of. (Jeremy Johns)**

exposure from top and bottom, the stone will then simply fall down as the wax holding it up burns away.

Other factors must also be considered, including making sure the stones do not touch each other. As the metal cools, it will contract, which may result in cracked stones. Intelligently spaced stones will prevent this. On the subject of stones, this is the most crucial factor within stone-in-place casting. While there is a little debate over which stones can survive the process, I genuinely would not stray from diamonds, rubies and sapphires. Cubic zirconia may also withstand the abuse. Be mindful when using stones with natural flaws as the heat involved can cause catastrophic failures. The same goes for using shaped stones, we all know that pointy bits are the weak point when pushing; the same can be said for thermal shock.

There is a reason why the likes of Polly Wales are so successful. Dedication to their craft and a great deal of effort has been invested into refining their process. They have tried and they have failed, probably on countless occasions. But just look at how incredible it can be when it's done right! You are not going to become brilliant overnight, but there's no harm in pushing boundaries like the other pioneers.

Electroforming

A special mention here for the absolutely bonkers but beautiful creations of Maud Traon. Electroforming is a process I have never ventured near, so I'm not going to try to explain how to do it! I'll most definitely let the visuals do the talking; Maud's jewellery often looks like it's from another planet! Without a doubt, it falls into the 'wearable art' category. Beautiful explosions of colour are mixed with rough stones, set in an unconventional manner. The end results can look beyond incredible, with great respect going to the maker for her dedication to design and unique craft.

GLOSSARY OF TERMS

Back cuts – Using a flat or round bottom scorper to raise a small notch of metal to hold stones in. Used by some setters to flush set (I do not like this), to lock stones in when setting from behind, and also used in setting claw clusters.

Backplate – A flat section of metal onto which a bezel setting is soldered.

Ball burr – A round cutting tool slotted into a pendant drill, which comes in various sizes and carries out a variety of tasks. These can include drilling out holes, seating stones and removing metal.

Bearer wire – A section of metal that is soldered into a tube, bezel or collet for a stone to sit on.

Bearing cutter – An angular cutting tool, slotted into a pendant drill, which comes in multiple sizes. Used for creating ridges underneath metal so stones can be slotted in, or engraving grooves in metal.

Bezel – A setting where the walls of the metal are pushed over the stone to secure it in place.

Bright cut – The art of using scorpers, gravers or burnishers to leave a crisp, shiny finish in various stone settings.

Burnisher – A narrow pointed tool (usually steel) used to smooth over metal, leaving behind a bright, shiny finish.

Cabochon – A smooth, polished stone with no facets. Rounded and domed on the top and flat on the bottom.

Calipers – A precision measuring tool, used to gauge various dimensions of materials. Usually digital these days, although some still swear by the old school analogue way.

Centre punch – A tool with a narrow, pointed nose, which is struck on the top with the intention of creating a mark in metal for precision drilling.

Channel setting – A method of setting where the stones are suspended within two walls by burring a ridge for them to slot into. The walls are then pushed over the stones.

Claw/prong setting – The most common style of setting. Stones are held in by various numbers (and styles of) claws after a seat is burred within them. The claws are finished decoratively to give a neat, pleasing finish.

Collet – A ring or rim of metal, designed to encircle the outside of a stone. The wall of the collet is pressed over onto the edge of the stone to set it. Can be handmade or pre-formed tube. *Also see:* Bezel.

Court shape – A ring that is slightly rounded on both the inside and outside, resulting in a comfortable fit.

Cross cut burr – A long, narrow burr (not tapered) that has teeth on the outside. Used to cut away metal in between stones for pavé and microclaw.

Cross technique – Using multiple styles of setting methods to achieve your goal.

Crown – The top part of a faceted stone, measured from the table to the girdle.

Culet – The very bottom point of a faceted gemstone.

Cup burr – A convex shaped burr, favoured by some setters to finish claws. However, can cause damage to stones.

'D' section – A ring that is curved on the outside but flat on the inside. The name comes from the 'D' shape cross-section the ring has.

Dop stick – A wooden dowel encased with setter's wax at the end to allow pieces to be held in for setting. Can be various sizes to accommodate different size jobs.

Faceted – A stone that has small flats polished onto it at regular and irregular intervals at precise angles. Great care is taken by polishers to achieve maximum effect from each stone.

Flash metal – Excess metal caused by burring or cutting away. A regular occurrence in stone setting.

Flat scorper – A narrow, sharp cutting tool. Has to be ground into shape and sharpened with a shallow angle. As the name suggests, has a flat bottom, like a mini chisel. Perfect for cutting metal away and creating bright cuts.

Flush setting – A setting method where the stone is 'sunk' into the surface, with the inside edge of the metal being pushed over and finished smooth and bright.

'Fried egg' effect – A common problem in pavé setting where a beader that is too small has been used in finishing. The centre is rounded and smooth, but the outer metal is squashed and splayed outwards, making it look like a cracked egg in a frying pan.

Gallery – A slice of metal that encircles and perfectly mirrors the shape of a stone, which then has claws attached to the outside. If single, the stone will use it as a seat. If double, the top gallery is used as a seat.

Girdle – The very outer rim of the stone where the crown meets the pavilion. Has to be covered (either entirely or at specific points) to secure the stone.

Goldilocks Rule – This is the most important law in stone setting! It comes up everywhere and is applied to every method in numerous situations. Don't sit the stone too deep, don't leave it too high… sit it somewhere in between. Don't leave the claw too long, don't cut it too short. Somewhere in the middle is ideal. And so on and so forth. A happy medium is often the place to be as a stone setter.

Grain/bead – A small section of metal, either 'raised' or left behind by precise cutting, which is then used to pavé set stones. After pushing, a concave beader or grain tool is used to round them off.

Inner/outer edge – This applies to the metal touching the stone and the metal where you've been pushing. Not every style has one or indeed both. They must each be crisp, flat and smooth. This is where a wobble or ripple can ruin hard effort and time.

Loupe/optivisors – Essential kit for stone setters. You cannot achieve any level of professional stone setting without magnification. You must become accustomed to using either regularly. If it looks perfect at x10, think how good it will appear to the naked eye!

Lozenge graver – A long, slender length of (usually) steel. Can be square or kite shape, but the cutting edge is always a point.

Microclaw – As the name suggests, this is claw setting at a very miniature level. It's a combination of multiple techniques, with the theory of claw and pavé joining forces to create their own baby. Metal is removed, leaving behind tiny claws to set the stone. Often decorative finishes are applied.

Millgrain – A row of tiny beads, used on the edge of a setting for decoration. Usually found on vintage jewellery, the technique is making a comeback in modern-day pieces.

Mohs Scale – Developed in 1812 by Friedrich Mohs, a German geologist. It is a scale of hardness used to determine how easily a stone can be scratched or scored. It has different degrees, in increasing hardness, ranging from talc (1) to diamond (10). Jewellers use it to determine just how careful they have to be when stone setting.

Multiple pavé – A style of pavé setting where stones are clustered together rather than in a straight line.

Pavilion – The bottom part of a faceted stone, measured from the girdle down to the culet.

Push tool – Whatever you use to set a stone into metal with. Usually home-made with a handle. An experienced setter will tailor theirs to their own needs, with it fitting their hand size and shape perfectly.

Raising the grain – Using a round-bottomed scorper to lift little flags of metal to create a grain or bead for pavé setting. This the old-fashioned method, with setters now preferring to cut away metal beforehand to create beads, rather than lifting metal and cutting afterwards.

Ring clamp – A tool used by a setter to hold rings (and other pieces) steady while setting. Usually a hinged section of wood with a wedge; however, more elaborate tools and clamps are now available to aide setting work.

Round scorper – A narrow, sharp cutting tool. Has to be ground into shape and sharpened with a shallow angle. As the name suggests, has a rounded bottom edge. Used to cut away metal, but also to raise the grain or create back cuts.

Rubover – *See* Chapter 2, Bezel Setting.

Safety-back file – A needle file with smooth edges and side opposite to where the cutting surface is. Ideal for finishing stone settings.

Saw cut – A cut taken through two separate sections of metal to achieve a flush join. From a setter's point of view, used when turning up a bezel setting to ensure a tight and secure solder join.

Scallop – A decorative 'scoop', filed out of metal in between claws to achieve a decorative finish. Used in microclaw setting.

Seat – Metal that the stone rests upon for setting.

Semi rubover – A bezel setting that has a gap exposing the sides of the stones. Not fully set, usually half set.

Setter's wax – Technically not wax, rather a resin-based substance that softens when gently heated. Similar to sealing wax used to close letters. Used to coat the end of a wooden dowel, which in turn can hold pieces of jewellery for setting.

Setting burr – A burr that is ideal for cutting seats for stones. Can be placed in a hand drill or pendant motor.

Sharing the bead – A term used in pavé setting, where a bead that is forced in between two stones to lock both into place touches both stones, hence 'sharing'.

Single row pavé – Pavé setting in a line, one after the other. Can be straight or on a curve.

Snipe nose pliers – Pliers that taper down to the nose, allowing them to reach into small spaces with precise results.

Spitzstick – A scorper used specifically for lining and removing metal. Narrows to a slender point, and is incredibly sharp.

Splitting the bead – A term used in pavé setting, where a bead is split in two and not only pushed in between two stones but also to either side over each stone. Different from sharing the bead.

Table – The top surface of a stone.

Tension set – A style of setting where a stone is held in by force between two sides of substantial metal.

Tube set – *See* Chapter 2, Bezel Setting.

'V' claw – A claw that is shaped and encases the point of a stone perfectly, rather than a round one.

Wall – The part of a bezel setting that is pushed over the stone.

ACKNOWLEDGEMENTS

There is only one person who truly deserves the biggest and loudest acknowledgement here... a huge shout out to Karen, my (long-suffering) wife and fiercest critic. The constant checking, then double-checking that things were sounding right, making sense or required at all, made sure this manual was finely tuned to the elevated level it turned out to be. I can be incredibly stubborn but Karen always knows how to get her point across and ensure I follow. Not only that, to have her patience and understanding when I lost myself deep inside Book-land rather than paying attention to her or my kids, Jake and Amy, was vital. It's down to her delicate mix of insistence and tolerance that this manual exists at all.

To my wonderful business partner, Ellie Smith-Barratt, a big thank you for putting up with me over these years! Going into business with someone that you've known as a close pal for nearly two decades is tricky, but we have most definitely made the most of it. Ellie is a steadying, calming influence on me and together, we are trying to make a real difference to people's lives here at Vanilla Ink. The story so far is one of success, and long may that continue! Also a big thank you to the team here at VIHQ and up at our second site in Banff. Jenna, Natasha, Annelies and Drew are a joy to work with and we wouldn't be where we are without them.

To my guinea pigs when writing this book, thank you. It was vital to get feedback from high-quality, experienced jewellers, and boy, did they respond. Some even sacrificed part of their weekends to check that everything made sense and was easy to follow! They were all speedy, thorough, and honest. Without their feedback, this book would have probably been an incomprehensible mess. It probably still is. A quick shout out to my non-jeweller eyes, too. These guys proofread for grammar and spelling but ended up proclaiming that they could now probably stone set proficiently just by reading alone! I'm taking that as a win.

Also to photographer extraordinaire, Stacey Bentley, who took my ridiculous curvy, sweeping jewellery and got the perfect angles! Her talent shines all the way through this manual, so a huge thank you to her. To all the incredible jewellers who gave us permission to use their images, I give an enormous thank you! We wanted this manual to have a truly international feel to it, and we reckon this has been delivered. From Scotland down to England, all the way around to Australia via Finland, The Netherlands and Lithuania. Then round to Mexico before landing back in Scotland again, we truly believe this represents the global jewellery family in the best way possible. Your beautiful jewellery is an example of perfectly executed stone setting.

Finally, where would this manual be without the beautiful and informative illustrations? These incredible works of art were all hand drawn by the ridiculously talented Jennifer Colquhoun, who was an absolute pleasure to work with. It was as if Jennifer could see inside my head and draw exactly what I was looking for. Her intricate detail dovetails perfectly with the text, her skill level is off the scale and I'm very jealous of her! Her work was vital to this manual, which is something I will always be grateful for.

INDEX

RELATED TITLES FROM CROWOOD

**Designing and Making
Glass Jewellery**
978 1 78500 677 7

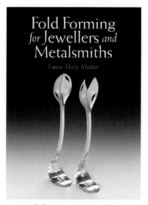

**Fold Forming for
Jewellers and
Metalsmiths**
978 1 78500 272 4

Glass Casting
978 1 78500 593 0

**Making Metal Clay
Jewellery**
978 1 78500 264 9

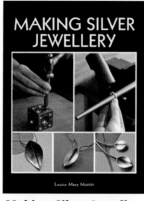

Making Silver Jewellery
978 1 84797 683 3

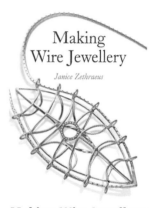

Making Wire Jewellery
978 1 78500 165 9

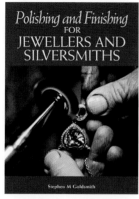

**Polishing and Finishing
for Jewellers
and Silversmiths**
978 1 78500 523 7

Quilling
978 1 78500 613 5

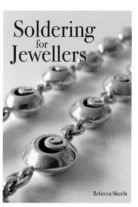

Soldering for Jewellers
978 1 78500 274 8